The Modern Creation Trilogy

Volume III

Society and Creation

The Modern Creation Trilogy

Volume III

Society and Creation

Dr. Henry M. Morris
Dr. John D. Morris

Master Books

First printing: November 1996

For information write: Master Books, Inc., P.O. Box 727, Green Forest, AR 72638.

ISBN: 0-89051-222-1

Acknowledgments

The writers would like to thank Mrs. Mary Ruth Smith, B.S. for typing and editing the manuscript, Mr. Merle Meeter for further editorial suggestions, and Dr. Larry Vardiman for reading the entire manuscript and making valuable suggestions regarding content.

Table of Contents

Introduction

"Be not deceived: evil communications corrupt good manners" (1 Cor. 15:33). Nowhere is this biblical maxim more relevant than in the influence of evolutionism in human society. The evolutionary deception and its evil influences have, indeed, corrupted every area of human life on this planet, and this fact in itself should be enough to demonstrate its ultimate satanic source. Evolutionism is a false religion, designed to turn men and women away from belief in the true God of creation and from participation in His wonderful gift of salvation and eternal life.

Volume 3 of this Trilogy is designed to show the age-long, pervasively evil, influence of evolutionism. In Volume 1 *(Scripture and Creation)*, it is shown that the Holy Scriptures, the inspired Word of God, clearly teach that all things were created, not evolved. Volume 2 *(Science and Creation)* demonstrates that all the *real facts* of science (as distinct from naturalistic speculations) likewise point to special creation, rather than evolution.

It is not surprising, therefore, that rejection of creation and the Creator in favor of evolutionary speculations will have a deadly impact upon society and all human relationships. The Lord Jesus reminds us that "a good tree bringeth not forth corrupt fruit; neither doth a corrupt tree bring forth good fruit" (Luke 6:43). The corrupt fruits of evolution prove beyond question that evolution is a corrupt tree with corrupt roots. Christians and others often try to pluck off and destroy the fruits of evolutionism (abortion, Communism, etc.), but they will merely grow back again, as long as the tree and its roots are left in the ground.

First, however, Christian believers and other concerned persons must be able to see that this is really the case. They need to be taught the true nature of evolutionism, with its long history and destructive influence on human life and society.

That is the main purpose of this volume, the third in what we have called "The Modern Creation Trilogy." First, we want to document the fact that evolutionism does, indeed, dominate our educational system and our whole society, being taught in practically every subject in the schools, as well as in all the news media and in our very political and legal structure.

We then must see also that it is not just a peripheral development in an increasingly secularized society. Evolutionism, in either atheistic or pantheistic form, has penetrated and dominated almost every religious, cultural, and political system throughout history. This insight will help us to understand the cosmic dimensions of the conflict of evolutionism with true creationism, and how we should respond to its application in the many problems of modern society.

Finally, we want to examine in some detail many of these problems and the impact of evolutionary thinking in aggravating them. This in turn will enable us to appreciate — and, it is hoped, implement — the salutary effect of applying creationist criteria to their solution.

That is the purpose of this particular volume. We shall begin, then, by showing how evolutionary philosophy does, indeed, pervade every discipline of modern education and communication.

Chapter 1

The Pervasive Influence of Evolutionism

For several decades after the Scopes trial, most people, including even most Bible-believing Christians, tended to regard the evolution-creation issue as one of very little importance. The question of uniformitarianism versus catastrophism, including whether the flood of Noah was worldwide or only local, was considered of even less importance.

These events of the far-off past, many felt, have no relevance to the pressing problems of the modern world, and therefore were matters of little concern to them. The questions could well be left to the professional geologists, in the case of uniformitarianism, and to the biologists, in the case of evolutionism. Even in the matter of Christian faith, the gospel of Christ did not then seem to depend upon any particular cosmological model; both evolutionists and creationists could believe in God and could be saved through personal faith in Jesus Christ, so the argument went. A person's relation to God and to his fellowmen did not depend upon whether he or she believed that the Flood was worldwide. If necessary, they felt, it would somehow be possible to reinterpret Genesis to correspond to the prescriptions of the evolutionary scientists without any particular damage to basic biblical philosophy and teaching.

It is this continuing attitude of indifference that is, if anything, more harmful to true faith, however, than even open hostility by the camp of atheism. It *does* make a tremendous difference what men believe about their origin, and the sad history of the Christian church of the past 150 years ought to be sufficient proof of this fact. The evolutionary-uniformitarian cosmology is far more than a mere biological or geological hypothesis. It is a complete world view, a comprehensive philosophy of life and meaning. One cannot really believe in an evolutionary *history* of the world without also believing in an evolutionary *future* of the world. A person's philosophy of origins will inevitably determine sooner or later what he believes concerning his destiny, and even what he believes about the meaning and purpose of his life and actions right now in the present world!

The doctrine of origins, indeed, is the foundation of every other doctrine. That, of course, is why God placed His revelation of origins in the first chapter of the Bible. Everything else in the Bible and in history is built upon this foundation. Once the foundations have been undermined, it is only a matter of time before the entire superstructure must collapse. Harvard biologist Dr. Ernst Mayr, one of the world's leading evolutionists, confirms this as follows:

> Since Darwin, every knowing person agrees that man is descended from the apes. . . . Evolution has an impact on every aspect of man's thinking: his philosophy, his metaphysics, his ethics. . . . Today, of course, there is no such thing as the theory of evolution; it is the fact of evolution. . . . The only arguments now are over technical problems, but the basic fact of evolution is so clearly established that no scientist worries about it any more.[1]

Professor Mayr is an outstanding scientist, probably one of the top half dozen or so evolutionary biologists in the world, but either his ignorance or arrogance is clearly showing in the above interview.

Thousands of well-qualified scientists in the world today are convinced creationists. One of these, Dr. Kenneth Cumming, who studied under Dr. Mayr at Harvard and received his Ph.D. degree in Dr. Mayr's department, is now dean of the Graduate School at the Institute for Creation Research (ICR). Another creationist scientist, Dr. Duane Gish, with a Ph.D. in biochemistry from the University of California (Berkeley) — a school with an equivalent reputation on the West Coast to that of Harvard on the East — clearly defeated Dr. Mayr in a written debate in *Nature* magazine several years before joining the ICR science staff. He has since participated in over 300 debates with leading evolutionary scientists, but neither Dr. Mayr nor any other Harvard evolutionist will condescend (dare) to debate him in public.

Dr. Mayr is right, however, in stating that evolution has infected every area of human thought, and is commonly taught in the schools and

[1] Ernst Mayr, "Interview" *Omni* (March/April 1988), p. 46.

colleges of the whole world as an established fact. As a leading socialist scholar (himself an evolutionist, though not a Darwinian evolutionist) he has said:

> Evolutionary theory has been enshrined as the centerpiece of our educational system, and elaborate walls have been erected around it to protect it from unnecessary abuse.[2]

With respect to God's role in the universe, the evolution model essentially eliminates it altogether (as practically all of the leaders of evolutionary thought believe), or at least relegates it to some external and innocuous supervision that can never be demonstrated or even studied in any scientific way. In an earlier article Mayr said this:

> Every anti-evolutionist prior to 1859 allowed for the intermittent, if not constant, interference by the Creator. The natural causes postulated by the evolutionists completely separated God from his creation, for all practical purposes. The new explanatory model replaced planned teleology by the haphazard process of natural selection. This required a new concept of God and a new basis for religion.[3]

At present, evolutionary thought is dominant not only in biology, but also in all other disciplines as well. The creationist cosmology has been held by only a small minority, and too few of these have had any substantial scientific comprehension of its implications.

One of the leading evolutionists of this century emphasized the universal scope of the evolutionary process as follows:

> Evolution comprises all the stages of the development of the universe: the cosmic, biological, and human or cultural developments. Attempts to restrict the concept of evolution to biology are gratuitous. Life is a product of the evolution of inorganic nature, and man is a product of the evolution of life.[4]

Another prominent proponent of evolutionary thought, Dr. William

---

[2] Jeremy Rifkin, *Algeny* (New York, NY: Viking Press, 1983), p. 112.

[3] Ernst Mayr, "The Nature of the Darwinian Revolution" *Science*, vol. 176 (June 2, 1972), p. 988.

[4] Theodosius Dobzhansky, "Changing Man," *Science*, vol. 155 (January 27, 1967), p. 409.

Provine of Cornell University, emphasizes the completely atheistic assumptions of the modern scientific establishment.

> Modern science directly implies that the world is organized strictly in accordance with deterministic principles or chance. There are no purposive principles whatsoever in nature. There are no gods and no designing forces that are detectable.[5]

Some even consider this approach to be a kind of a game they must play in order to be *accepted* as scientists.

> Operational science takes no position about the existence or non-existence of the supernatural; only that this factor is not to be invoked in scientific explanations.[6]

No creationist scientist, of course, would ever invoke miracles to explain natural phenomena that can be observed in operation today, although evolutionists often imply that this is what we do. But "operational science" is altogether different from what some have called "origins' science." There is no way that the origin of the universe or of life or of the various major kinds of life can ever be observed or tested in the field or in the laboratory today. That being so, there is no reason whatever *not* to invoke the supernatural to explain origins — especially when (as shown compellingly in Volume 2 of this trilogy) presently *observable* processes do not **originate** anything. But that's the game evolutionists play!

The Biological Sciences

That biology is dominated by evolutionism today goes almost without saying. Such scientists as those cited above (e.g., Mayr, Dobzhansky, Dickerson) are biologists. Note also the statement below by Dr. Provine, stressing that not only are biologists evolutionists, but also, in almost all cases, atheists.

---

[5] William B. Provine, "Progress in Evolution and Meaning in Life," in *Evolutionary Progress,* ed. Matthew H. Nitecki, (Chicago, IL: University of Chicago Press, 1988), p. 65.

[6] Richard E. Dickerson, "The Game of Science," *Perspectives on Science and Faith*, vol. 44 (June 1992), p. 137. Dr. Dickerson was a member of the team of scientists on the accreditation team that tried unsuccessfully in 1989 to close down the ICR Graduate School because we would not play this game. He stated that even if we met all other criteria, our programs should not be approved as long as we persisted in teaching science in a creationist context, even though the ICR Graduate School was a private school receiving no money from federal, state, or local governments.

> Very few truly religious biologists remain. Most are atheists, and many have been driven there by their understanding of the evolutionary process and other sciences.[7]

Probably the area of biology of greatest interest to most people is that of anthropology, the study of man and his life processes, especially his origin.

The accepted theory of man's development leaves no room for the biblical Adam, but rather visualizes a gradual divergence of man and the apes from an unknown common ancestor perhaps in the Pliocene Epoch or earlier, with man finally evolving into essentially his present form perhaps about a million years ago. Human evolution is insisted upon as factual, not even open to question.

> That man has evolved from less distinguished ancestors is indisputable. What we are concerned with is not to show where man came from. That we no longer doubt. But to show how he came; to show the processes by which ape-like animals became men.[8]

It is hardly necessary to point out the profound influence of evolution on the study of life processes. It is here, in biology, that organic evolution is best known. All standard biology textbooks today are structured entirely around the evolutionary model, and this is true at every grade level. Life is always presented as having evolved by natural processes from non-life, all the various higher forms of life from simpler forms, and finally man himself as the highest product of the evolutionary process to date. Whether the particular study is botany, zoology, genetics, ecology, embryology, or any of the other many branches of biological science, the underlying philosophy is always that of evolution!

The Physical Sciences

The physical sciences are as much affected today by evolutionary thinking as are the life sciences. Even physics is influenced a great deal by cosmogonic speculations.

> Modern astrophysics has brought a new aspect to physics: the historical perspective. Previously, physics was the science of things as they are: now, astrophysics deals with the development of stars and galaxies, with the formation of the

---

[7] Provine, "Progress in Evolution," p. 68.

[8] C. D. Darlington, *The Evolution of Man and Society* (New York, NY: Simon & Schuster, 1970), p. 32, 21.

> elements, with the expanding universe. . . stars are formed from a hydrogen cloud, elements are formed by synthesis from hydrogen, and stars are developing through different states.[9]

Even in such fields as mathematics and technology, the authors of textbooks commonly feel it necessary to begin their treatments with their own purely imaginary speculations about how their particular field of technology first evolved. For example, a popular mathematics book begins thus:

> In the beginning, there were no numbers; or, if there were, primitive man was unaware of them. Whether the numbers were always "there" (where?) or had to be invented, has been a much discussed question, and we shall leave it to the philosophers to continue that discussion without our aid. What we can say with some assurance is that the ability to count came relatively late to civilization.[10]

Almost all astronomers, astrophysicists, and cosmologists today seem at least to be practical atheists, diligently seeking to explain even the origin of the universe itself without God. It evolved out of nothing but the mathematics of quantum physics and relativity theory, not requiring any kind of cause at all, so they say!

> Thus we reach a general conclusion: there is no philosophy of big bang cosmology that makes it reasonable to reject the fundamental thesis of big bang cosmology: that the universe began to exist without a cause.[11]

Herein is a most marvelous thing! The fundamental premise of science is that every effect must have an adequate cause. Yet the greatest "effect" of all — the mighty universe itself — had no Cause to produce it. It just happened!

Not only did the universe evolve out of nothing. From that remarkable beginning, the basic elements, the stars, the galaxies, the planets, and even living organisms — as well as everything else — have

---

[9] Victor K. Weisskopf, "Physics in the Twentieth Century," *Science*, vol. 168 (May 22, 1970), p. 929-930.

[10] C. S. Ogilvey and John L. Anderson, *Excursions in Number Theory* (New York, NY: Oxford University Press, 1966), p. 1.

[11] Quentin Smith, "Did the Big Bang have a Cause?" *British Journal of Philosophy of Science*, vol. 45 (1994), p. 666.

evolved from that primeval "happening," according to our evolutionist astronomers, physicists, and chemists, as pointed out by Professor Weisskopf above.

Lest anyone think that the above scenario is merely a creationist plot to make evolutionists seem ridiculous, consider one more quotation from an evolutionary humanistic scientist.

> So what had to happen to start the universe was the formation of an empty bubble of highly curved space-time. How did this bubble form? What caused it? Not everything requires a cause. It could have just happened spontaneously as one of the many linear combinations of universes that has the quantum numbers of the void. . . . Our universe is a very unlikely one, but it is the only one we have. And this unlikeliness of our universe is no argument for it having been planned.[12]

Well, then, what is the evidence that it was *not* planned? Again, let Dr. Stenger answer:

> Much is still in the speculative stage, and I must admit that there are yet no known empirical or observational tests that can be used to test the idea of an accidental origin.[13]

It would, indeed, be difficult to devise a test that could observe something impossible happening in the non-observable, non-repeatable past! Dr. Stenger is modest enough to "admit" that.

In any case, it is certain that evolutionism dominates the physical sciences today just as much as the biological sciences.

The Earth Sciences

As far as geology and the other earth sciences are concerned (e.g., paleontology), the situation is similar to that in the physical sciences. Those aspects of geology that deal with *present* phenomena and processes (just as in physics and chemistry) are carried out without regard to the *origin* of the processes or systems. When, however, geologists venture into *historical* geology (that is, the origin and development of the earth during the assumed geological ages), their science is also fully dominated by evolutionism. This aspect is especially dominant in paleontology, of course.

> Historic geology relies chiefly on paleontology, the

---

[12] Victor L. Stenger, "Was the Universe Created?" *Free Inquiry* (Summer 1987), p. 29.
[13] *Ibid.*, p. 30.

> study of fossil organisms. . . . The geologist utilizes knowledge of organic evolution, as preserved in the fossil record, to identify and correlate the lithic records of ancient time.[14]

This particular quotation is from an older, much-used, textbook, but the situation is no different today. Indeed, it is so widely known that *all* the natural sciences — biological, physical, and geological — are everywhere today structured within an evolutionary framework that even this brief documentation may seem redundant.

It may *not* be so widely recognized, however, that even the social sciences and humanities are permeated with evolutionism — possibly even more so than the natural sciences. Therefore, we need especially to look at these.

The Social Sciences

As an introduction to the impact of evolutionism on the whole field of modern so-called "liberal arts," the following evaluation appeared recently in what is probably the most influential weekly in the entire field of higher education:

> The social and conceptual revolution that we are now witnessing . . . can be traced back to Darwin. The cultural holists . . . are using evolutionary and ecological concepts to explain social conflict and social change. As revolutionary as their work may appear to conservative scholars, it is grounded in the evolutionary model that scientists no longer question.[15]

When one turns to the social sciences, it is soon apparent that these have been more influenced by evolutionary thought than even the biological sciences. Psychology, the study of the mind, is almost entirely based on the assumption that man is only an animal, derived by evolutionary descent from an ape-like ancestor. This was the view of Sigmund Freud, who has exerted probably the greatest single influence on the structure of modern psychology. It is a common saying that, as Darwin banished God from life, Freud drove Him from the soul. Freud's proverbial emphasis upon the "unconscious" and on uninhibited sexual freedom were both based squarely upon man's supposed brute ancestry.

---

[14] O. D. von Engeln and K. E. Caster, *Geology* (New York, NY: McGraw-Hill Publishers, 1952), p. 423.

[15] Betty Jean Craige, "The Pursuit of Truth is Inherently Disruptive and Anti-Authoritarian," *Chronicle of Higher Education* (January 6, 1993), p. A56.

The same can be said in varying degrees about the contributions of James, Watson, Jung, Skinner, and other founders and leaders of psychology, including the so-called humanistic psychologists of the present day. Dr. Rene Dubos of the Rockefeller Institute, in a national Sigma Xi–Phi Beta Kappa lecture, noted this as follows:

> Many aspects of human behavior which appear incomprehensible, or even irrational, become meaningful when interpreted as survivals of attributes which were useful when they first appeared during evolutionary development and which have persisted because the physical evolution of man came to a relative halt about 150,000 years ago. Phenomena ranging all the way from the aberrations of mob psychology to the useless disturbances of metabolism and circulation which occur during verbal conflicts at the office or at a cocktail party are as much the direct consequences of the stimuli which were their immediate causes. The urge to control property and to dominate one's peers are also forms of territoriality and dominance among most if not all animal societies.[16]

Even the apparent intelligence and purposeful actions which are characteristic of man are believed to be merely products of the random, purposeless evolutionary process. Dr. Hudson Hoagland, then president of the American Academy of Arts and Sciences, said this, for example:

> But man himself and his behavior are an emergent product of purely fortuitous mutations and evolution by natural selection acting upon them. Non-purposive natural selection has produced purposive human behavior.[17]

Such writers rarely bother to concern themselves about the obvious contradiction of these concepts with the scientific law of cause and effect, since they regard evolution as simply having in some mysterious way transcended this law. In short, with the exception of a very small minority today, the professions of psychology and psychiatry are characterized by a strong commitment to evolution and by animosity toward biblical Christianity.

Turning to the field of sociology, one quickly discovers that the

---

[16] Rene Dubos, "Humanistic Biology," *American Scientist*, vol. 43 (March 1965), p. 10-11.

[17] Hudson Hoagland, "Science and the New Humanism," *Science*, vol. 143 (January 10, 1964), p. 113.

study of man's cultures and societies is universally cast in the same mold as the study of his presumed biological evolution.

> A second kind of evolution is psycho-social or cultural evolution. This is unique to man. Its history is very recent; it started roughly a million years ago with our hominid tool-making ancestors. . . . In the last 300 years the ever-accelerating developments through science are a continuation of this psycho-social evolution, which, in terms of progress, is thousands of times faster than biological evolution resulting from genetic mutations.[18]

Similarly, one of the leading social scientists of the past half century, Dr. Harry Elmer Barnes, has said this:

> Unquestionably the most potent influences contributing to the rise and development of truly historical sociology were Spencer's theory of cosmic evolution and the Darwinian doctrine of organic evolution and their reactions upon social science.[19]

Moreover, Alan Lomax of the Bureau of Applied Social Research at Columbia University, concluded an important worldwide study of cultural characteristics as follows:

> For almost a century, the intellectual atmosphere of the world has been poisoned by a false Darwinism that judged human social development as the survival of the fittest — that is, of the most successfully aggressive individuals and societies.[20]

It is a matter of great concern to Christian parents and pastors that evolution is taught as fact in practically all public schools and at all grade levels. Science and social studies textbooks invariably support evolution. It is encouraging that organized opposition to this clearly unfair and unconstitutional state of affairs has developed in practically every state, with strong citizens' groups advocating a return to a more balanced approach to the study of origins. It is not as well-known, however, that not only in organized courses, but even in the very philosophy and

---

[18] *Ibid.*

[19] Harry Elmer Barnes, *Historical Sociology* (New York, NY: The Philosophical Library, 1948), p. 13.

[20] Alan Lomax, with Norman Berkowitz, "The Evolutionary Taxonomy of Culture," *Science*, vol. 177 (July 22, 1972), p. 239.

methodology of the entire public education approach, evolutionary assumptions have been at the foundation. The curricular content, the "self-discovery" emphasis on social change, and many other aspects of modern educationism are founded on evolutionary assumptions. The determinative influence of John Dewey and his disciples on modern education, of course, speaks for itself.

Modern textbooks of world history almost invariably begin with the standard evolutionary development of the world and man, supplemented by the evolutionary interpretation of developing nations, races, and classes. This kind of approach was, of course, made to order for the Marxist and Nazi distortions of history, as will be discussed shortly. Even apart from these, however, historical interpretations today are thoroughly permeated with evolutionary assumptions. Therefore, H. J. Muller, in speculating about pre-historical cultural development, once said:

> Another factor that must have facilitated cultural evolution in the past is a kind of non-genetic natural selection operating between different groups, and between portions of a group, so as to favor more the continuance and spread of those whose cultures were more conducive to their own survival and increase.[21]

It is also well-known that the most influential of our modern historians, men such as Charles Beard and Arnold Toynbee, have uniformly been committed to doctrinaire evolutionary concepts of history, both ancient and modern.

There are, of course, a great many different philosophies, but all of them — except a genuine biblical philosophy — are evolutionary philosophies. Most of those now prominent are essentially variant forms of naturalism. The philosophies of Karl Marx and Friedrich Nietzsche — the forerunners of Stalin and Hitler — have been particularly baleful in their effects. Both were dedicated evolutionists. Perhaps the most influential American philosopher was John Dewey, and his philosophy also was built on Darwinism and pantheistic humanism.

> Dewey was the first philosopher of education to make systematic use of Darwin's ideas.[22]

The humanities include literature and the fine arts, as well as

[21] H. J. Muller, "Human Values in Relation to Evolution," *Science*, vol. 127 (March 21, 1958), p. 628.

[22] Christian O. Weber, *Basic Philosophies of Education* (New York, 1960), p. 252.

philosophy and history. There is such a gulf between the sciences and the humanities that they have actually been widely referred to as the "two cultures." However, in terms of the basic world views which they hold, they are one. The humanities, no less than the natural sciences and the social sciences, regard man as the naturalistic product of his environment. The philosophy, morality, esthetics, and other aspects of modern humanism all are rooted in naturalism and evolutionism.

> Evolutionary concepts are applied also to social institutions and the arts. Indeed, most political parties, as well as schools of theology, sociology, history, or arts, teach these concepts and make them the basis of their doctrines. Thus, theoretical biology now pervades all of western culture indirectly through the concept of progressive historical change.[23]

One need only explore modern literature, listen to modern music, watch modern drama, or view modern art to become quickly convinced that they are all pervaded (and perverted) by a spirit of amoralism and atheism that can be grounded only in the belief that science has proved that man is an animal and God is dead.

Ethics and Religion

Once man has rejected the Bible and other religious authority, there is no more divine constraint toward honesty or purity or charity or any of the other ethical values associated with divine revelation.

> An ethical system that bases its premises on absolute pronouncements will not usually be acceptable to those who view human nature by evolutionary criteria.[24]

Nevertheless, man cannot survive in chaos and anarchy, and, therefore, he must have some kind of ethical standard. Since "science" has taken away his former guide, many scientists feel constrained to provide, in substitution, a new "scientific ethics," and the scientific journals frequently carry articles devoted to this theme.

And what is the basis of this scientific ethics? Why, evolution, of course!

> Moreover, scientific thought and its devotion to truth are themselves a product of the evolutionary process, and must therefore have proved themselves, hitherto at any

---

[23] Rene Dubos, "Humanistic Biology," p. 6.

[24] Arno G. Motulsky, "Brave New World?" *Science*, vol. 185 (August 23, 1974), p. 654.

rate, to have survival value.[25]

In fact, there seems to be an increasing clamor from evolutionary scientists that they could and should direct future evolution and human societies in accord with their concept of a scientific evolutionary system of ethics. H. J. Muller affirms this:

> It is high time for modern man, everywhere, again to revise his concepts of values, in accord with the utterly new view that science, and especially evolutionary science, has given him of the nature of the world and of his actual and potential relations to it.[26]

Two leading evolutionists have expressed cogently what most of them believe. Ethical systems have no basis in divine revelation; they are merely products of natural selection:

> Morality, or more strictly our belief in morality, is merely an adaptation put in place to further our reproductive ends. . . . In an important sense, ethics as we understand it is an illusion fobbed off on us by our genes to get us to cooperate.[27]

Even the ethical norms incorporated in religious systems are said to be merely a product of evolutionary struggle in the past. A prominent "religious" member of the Dead Sea Scrolls editing team has said this:

> For what religious man came eventually to think of as "conscience" is simply the faculty that enabled his hominid ancestors to inhibit their programmed response to stimuli in the interests of some longer-term advantage. "Guilt" is the unease that accompanies and sometimes motivates that control, and "god" is the idealist projection of the conscience in moral terms.[28]

Almost a hundred years ago John Dewey, the architect of our modern system of public education, gave a profoundly influential address on the subject of evolution and ethics. He climaxed his presentation with the following sweeping generalizations:

---

[25] Walter R. Brain, "Science and Antiscience," *Science*, vol. 148 (April 9, 1965), p. 197.

[26] H. J. Muller, "Human Values in Evolution," p. 628.

[27] Michael Ruse and Edward O. Wilson, "Evolution and Ethics," *New Scientist*, vol. 203 (October 17, 1985), p. 51.

[28] John Allegro, "Divine Discontent," *American Atheist*, vol. 28 (September 1986), p. 26.

> There are no doubt sufficiently profound distinctions between the ethical process and the cosmic process as it existed prior to man and to the formation of human society. So far as I know, however, all of these differences are summed up in the fact that the process and the forces bound up with the cosmic have come to consciousness in man. That which was instinct in the animal is conscious impulse in man. That which was "tendency to vary" in the animal is conscious foresight in man. That which was unconscious adaptation and survival in the animal, taking place by the "cut and try" method until it worked itself out, is with man conscious deliberation and experimentation. That this transfer from unconsciousness to consciousness has immense importance, need hardly be argued. It is enough to say that it means the whole distinction of the moral from the unmoral.[29]

Long ago, Thomas Henry Huxley, the famous evolutionary propagandist, clearly recognized that evolutionary history implied a basic principle in nature of aggressive self-interest. The great evolutionary slogans of the time — "struggle for existence" and "survival of the fittest" — clearly suggested a naturalistic ethic that continually pitted individuals, races, species, classes, and nations against each other. Huxley also saw that this system squarely contradicted the Christian ethic, and made this the theme of his Romanes lectures, *Evolution and Ethics*. In the present century, one of the leading evolutionists of the interwar period, Sir Arthur Keith, published another influential book with the same title. The entire volume amplifies and reinforces the theme of Huxley; namely, that the ethics taught by Christ and by evolution are polar opposites. Among other things, he argued that:

> If the final purpose of our existence is that which has been and is being worked out under the discipline of evolutionary law, then, although we are quite unconscious of the end result, we ought, as Dr. Waddington has urged, to help on "that which tends to promote the ultimate course of evolution." If we do so, then we have to abandon the hope of ever attaining a universal system of ethics; for, as we have just seen, the ways of national evolution, both in the past and in the present, are cruel, brutal, ruthless, and without mercy.[30]

[29] John Dewey, "Evolution and Ethics," reprinted in *Scientific Monthly* (February 1954), p. 66. Originally published in *The Monist*, vol. 8 (1897-1901).

Sir Arthur adds another interesting observation with the following:

> It was often said in 1914 that Darwin's doctrine of evolution had bred war in Europe, particularly in Germany. An expression of this belief is still to be met with. In 1935 a committee of psychologists, representing thirty nations, issued a manifesto in which it was stated that "war is the necessary outcome of Darwin's theory. . . ." The law of evolution, as formulated by Darwin, provides an explanation of wars between nations, the only reasonable explanation known to me.[31]

Of course, the Christian would say, rather, that wars result from sin, and that the only hope for permanent peace is in Jesus Christ. But it is clear that the inexorable logic of evolutionary reasoning leads directly to the conclusion that war and struggle are the chief good, leading to evolutionary advance:

> Meantime, let me say that the conclusion I have come to is this: the law of Christ is incompatible with the law of evolution — as far as the law of evolution has worked hitherto. Nay, the two laws are at war with each other; the law of Christ can never prevail until the law of evolution is destroyed.[32]

Now, admittedly, such views are not shared by most modern evolutionists, especially in America, where war suddenly became unpopular during the Viet-Nam conflict. Nevertheless, Sir Arthur was recognized by many to be one of the greatest evolutionists of modern times, and he had given more study to this subject of evolutionary ethics than any of his contemporaries. Many modern evolutionists like to stress "cooperation" as a viable force in evolutionary advance, but they do so without much conviction. Even such a cautious scientist as Dr. Frederick Seitz, when serving as president of the National Academy of Sciences, said the following:

> We can, of course, be grateful to nature for the highly remarkable genetic gifts which we have inherited as a result of the very complex process of selection which our ancestors experienced. We must also keep in mind, however, that

---

[30] Sir Arthur Keith, *Evolution and Ethics* (New York, NY: Putnam, 1947), p. 15.
[31] *Ibid.*, p. 149.
[32] *Ibid.*, p. 15.

> many of our most valued characteristics probably emerged out of interhuman competition. We probably have instinctive patterns of behavior which are fundamentally inimical to human cooperation on an indefinitely broad scale.[33]

Not even the domain of religion has escaped the influence of evolution. We should remember the classic diatribe of Sir Julian Huxley, who could probably be justly identified as the world's premier evolutionist of the 20th century. As the keynote speaker at the great Darwinian Centennial Convocation in 1959 at the University of Chicago, he orated as follows:

> In the evolutionary system of thought there is no longer need or room for the supernatural. The earth was not created; it evolved. So did all the animals and plants that inhabit it, including our human selves, mind and soul, as well as brain and body. So did religion. Evolutionary man can no longer take refuge from his loneliness by creeping for shelter into the arms of a divinized father figure whom he himself has created.[34]

Of course, with the weight of all the leading scientific authorities on the side of evolution, religious leaders around the world have felt it necessary to devise systems for accommodating their faiths within the evolutionary framework. This has been a relatively easy adjustment for most of the non-Christian religions, which were all fundamentally evolutionary systems anyway.

Buddhism and Hinduism, with their doctrines of *karma* and their pantheistic conceptions of God; Confucianism and Taoism, with their essentially agnostic attitude toward the idea of a personal God; and Shintoism, with its deification of man and the state, are all fundamentally evolutionist in philosophy, so they quickly and easily adapted themselves to the Darwinian approach within the framework of their own systems.

The same is true of the animistic faiths, whenever their practitioners become sufficiently sophisticated in their understanding of the modern world through education (often, sad to say, provided by "Christian" nations, and even sometimes in missionary schools). Fundamentalist missionaries in Africa and other areas of tribal religions report that the

---

[33] Frederick Seitz, "Science and Modern Man," *American Scientist*, vol. 54 (September 1966), p. 230.

[34] Sir Julian Huxley, *Associated Press* dispatch (November 27, 1959).

teaching of evolution in the schools, together with its adaptation as a veneer over revived demon worship, is today one of the most serious hindrances to the gospel in such lands.

In their primitive form (or, better, degenerate forms, as derived from primitive monotheism in the manner described by the Bible in Rom. 1:18-32), these animistic religions are themselves crudely evolutionist, all believing in some form of magical development of the first men and animals from previous materials. Though they retain in some cases a very faint and impersonal tribal memory of a "high God" of some sort, their practical daily religion has to do altogether with the physical world and its control by the spirits of departed ancestors and demons.

Modern spiritism is essentially the same thing, and this popular religion, together with its varied, associated cults — astrology, witchcraft, satanism, theosophy, Zen Buddhism, and the like — has been in recent years sweeping like wildfire over the world, especially Europe and Latin America. In spite of their individual differences, all such occult religions uniformly make the claim that they are more in accord with the modern scientific evolutionary view of the world than are the traditional religions, especially Christianity, calling themselves religions of the "New Age."

Even the various pseudo-Christian cults, such as Christian Science, Unity, and others of that kind have commonly accepted evolution into their systems. In somewhat analogous fashion, the parabiblical religions of Judaism and Islam, though nominally committed to faith in the Genesis account of creation, have now largely capitulated to the evolutionary cosmology in their philosophies. Reformed Judaism and Conservative Judaism have almost completely accepted Darwinian evolution and the higher critical views of the Old Testament, and even many Orthodox Jews have adopted a symbolic interpretation of the Genesis record.

The Muslim religious leaders have largely done the same, although there are "fundamentalist" groups who adhere to the literal creation of all things in the beginning by Allah. The Muslim mystics and philosophers, with their wholly transcendent view of God's nature and their subjective approach to religious experience, have, in fact, for all practical purposes been evolutionary pantheists all along.

In general, it is realistic to say that nearly the whole world of religion — Christian, non-Christian, and quasi-Christian alike — has accepted the evolutionary cosmology in one form or another.

Some uninformed Christians might object that, surely, Christian people still reject evolution. However, this is not true at all, at least for the majority of Christian self-styled "intellectuals," and many others who follow their lead.

The history of organized Christianity in the past century has been in large measure a sad record of compromise and retreat before the attacks of the evolutionists. In the 19th century, the so-called "higher criticism" launched its attacks against the authenticity of the Old Testament, especially the books of Moses, leading to the "documentary hypothesis" of the composition of the Old Testament writings. Many conservative seminaries and Bible schools today devote much study to the refutation of this higher criticism, but they ignore the evolutionary philosophy that spawned it.

> Sometimes people talk as though the "higher criticism" of texts in recent times has had more influence than the higher criticism of nature. This seems to me to be nonsense. The higher criticism has been simply an application of an awakened critical faculty to a particular kind of material, and was encouraged by the achievement of this faculty to form its bold conclusions. If the biologists, the geologists, the astronomers, and the anthropologists, had not been at work, I venture to think that the higher critics would have been either non-existent or a tiny minority in a world of fundamentalists.[35]

Even Bible-believing Christians who reject the higher-critical views of Genesis have again and again tried to compromise with evolution by novel exegetical twists of Genesis. This is always only a superficial and temporary stratagem, and it inevitably culminates in a reinterpretation of the entire Christian faith to correlate with the full-orbed evolutionary view of the world and society. Today, almost all of the colleges and seminaries of the large denominations, even those that are assumed to be conservative, have incorporated the evolutionary system and its associated liberal or neo-orthodox theology into their teachings.

Moreover, many schools that until recent years were strongly fundamental and anti-evolutionary are now allowing theistic evolution (or its semantic substitute, progressive creation) as a legitimate position for their faculty to teach if they so choose. This compromise has already in many instances been followed by a weakened doctrine of biblical inspiration, and increased conformity to the world in areas of morals and social activism.

---

[35] F. M. Powicke, *Modern Historians and the Study of History, Essays* (London, 1955), p. 228.

The documentation in this chapter could easily be multiplied many-fold.[36] What has been included, however, should certainly confirm the fact that evolutionism is not a peripheral matter of concern to only a few specialists. The fact is that evolutionary thought is of paramount and fundamental importance in every field of science and education today. Christians ignore it or compromise with it only at great peril to their faith and that of their children. The anomaly here is that it is so widely accepted as truth, when it contradicts all revelation in Scripture, as well as all the real facts of science (see Volumes 1 and 2 of this Trilogy). Finally, as shown later in this volume, it has also done tremendous harm through all its societal implications and applications.

---

[36] See the Henry M. Morris' book *The Long War against God* (Grand Rapids, MI: Baker Book House, 1989), p. 17-52, for further discussion and documentation of the pervasive (and pernicious) influence of evolution in science and education.

Chapter 2

The Long History of Evolutionism

In order really to understand the amazingly pervasive influence of evolutionism in the world today, as discussed in the preceding chapter, we also must understand and appreciate its long and widespread influence in past history. Evolutionism definitely did not begin with Charles Darwin, as most people assume today.

The Darwinian Century

In the previous chapter we have traced the extensive influence of the evolutionary philosophy as it has affected almost every discipline and segment of modern culture, especially in the educational system. Obviously, such profound and widespread effects must have an adequate background cause. This did not all happen by chance, nor did it develop overnight. There has been a long history of evolutionary thought, and there have been powerful forces at work to bring about its universal acceptance. Especially must this be true in view of the fact that both the inspired Word of God and all the real data of science support creation rather than evolution. In this chapter, therefore, we shall in outline fashion attempt to trace some of this history, especially the pre-Darwinian history, of evolution.

The theory of evolution as held today is, of course, associated most commonly with Charles Darwin. It is doubtful whether any other scientist has ever received as much praise and adulation as has Darwin. He was even honored in what amounted almost to a religious worship service in a great convocation held in 1959 at the University of Chicago, on the occasion of the 100th anniversary of the publication of his famous book *The Origin of Species by Natural Selection.* On the anniversary year of his death (1982) there was another outpouring of ritual praise.

And yet the actual scientific accomplishments of Charles Darwin were relatively insignificant, at least by modern standards. The only college degree he earned was in theology, and that was based on a very undistinguished record. He was not inclined toward a career as a clergyman, and was in fact only a nominal believer in Christianity, at most. He became a biologist more or less by accident, spending five years on an extended voyage around the world as a ship's naturalist on the *Beagle*. This voyage began in 1831 when he was only 22 years old. It was at this time that he read Lyell's *Principles of Geology*, which, added to his previous reading of Thomas Malthus' *Principles of Population* and his own observations on the fauna of the South Pacific islands, eventually led to his full acceptance of evolution and his postulation of natural selection as its mechanism.

Darwin also published studies on barnacles, vegetable mold, and other more restricted biological subjects, but these were hardly of great significance. It was clearly his *Origin of Species* which acquired for him his super-reputation.

This situation is odd, however, for Charles Darwin certainly was not the inventor of the theory of evolution, as many suppose.

> The idea of evolution had been widespread for more than 100 years before 1859. Evolutionary interpretations were advanced increasingly often in the second half of the 18th and the first half of the 19th centuries.[1]

Neither did Darwin originate the idea of natural selection, although this was his frequent boast. As a matter of fact, he rushed his book into print before he was ready (although he had been working on it for well over 20 years), in the fear that Alfred Wallace would publish his own identical theory first:

> Wallace independently achieved and set forth the same ideas as Darwin. He was an independent discoverer of natural selection.[2]

For that matter, at least ten other writers are known to have discussed the concept of natural selection before either Darwin or Wallace did so.

---

[1] Ernst Mayr, "The Nature of the Darwinian Revolution" *Science*, vol. 176 (June 2, 1972), p. 981.

[2] Loren C. Eiseley, "Alfred Russel Wallace," *Scientific American*, vol. 200 (February 1959), p. 70.

Nevertheless, Darwin's renowned book *The Origin of Species by Natural Selection* was published in 1859 and immediately created a storm of controversy that has continued for more than 135 years! It is an interesting comment on the temper of the times, and of man's eagerness to discover a justifiable excuse for rejecting God as his Creator, that the first edition of the *Origin* was sold out before it was published.

Despite considerable opposition at first, Darwin's theories were soon largely accepted, both by scientists and religionists. The post-Darwinian century has beyond doubt, almost from the first, been one in which evolutionary thought has reigned virtually unchallenged. There have been so many volumes written on this subject that it is essentially common knowledge.

The most significant fact about Darwin is not his stature as a scientist but his influence as a symbol. His contribution came at just the right time to catalyze an explosive reaction, transforming in one generation a society that was already seething with inner rebellion against the predominant theological and biblical view of the world, into a humanity in open and often violent rebellion against its Creator.

Darwin has often been called the "Newton of biology," but Jacques Barzun showed that this was a "very loose description indeed." Barzun (professor of history and dean of the Graduate Faculties at Columbia University for many years) noted:

> Darwin was not a thinker and he did not originate the ideas that he used. He vacillated, added, retracted, and confused his own traces. As soon as he crossed the dividing line between the realm of events and the realm of theory he became "metaphysical" in the bad sense. His power of drawing out the implications of his theories was at no time very remarkable, but when it came to the moral order it disappeared altogether, as that penetrating evolutionist, Nietzsche, observed with some disdain.[3]

Nevertheless, despite Darwin's serious deficiencies as a scientist, thinker, and writer, Barzun also acknowledged his unprecedented influence.

> Clearly, both believers and unbelievers in natural selection agreed that Darwinism had succeeded as an orthodoxy, as a rally point for innumerable scientific,

---

[3] Jacques Barzun, *Darwin, Marx, Wagner*, 2nd ed. (Garden City, NY: Doubleday and Co., 1959), p. 84.

> philosophical, and social movements. Darwin had been the oracle and the *Origin of Species* the "fixed point with which evolution moved the world."[4]

Nevertheless, as we trace the history of the development and influence of evolutionary thought, it becomes evident that neither Charles Darwin nor his famous book provides the answer. We must look deeper and further than Darwin to find the real roots of evolutionism and its worldwide influence.

Why Darwin?

Although the name of Charles Darwin is honored — in fact almost revered by many — as the founder of the modern theory of evolution, it is largely an artificial and manufactured identification. As we have just noted, his name serves a purpose as a sort of symbol and rallying point for evolutionists, but his actual scientific accomplishments were rather ordinary and unimpressive by modern standards. Although many intellectuals seem to feel that it is sort of a union card to pay homage to him, one senses in their writings a feeling that they are not comfortable with this nor quite clear what it is that they admire in Darwin and his work. There seems to be something in these responses that has never yet been satisfactorily understood or explained. In fact, a leading modern evolutionist reminds us:

> Darwin . . . never really addressed the "origin of species" in his book of that title.[5]

The theory of evolution did not originate with Charles Darwin, of course, as noted above. Various evolutionary concepts were accepted by many people long before Darwin. His main contribution was the theory of natural selection as an evolutionary mechanism, but even this was not original with him. In an authoritative review of the origins of Darwinism, an eminent British biologist asserts the following:

> As to the means of transformation, however, Erasmus Darwin originated almost every idea that has since appeared in evolutionary theory. . . . All three men (i.e., William C. Wells, James C. Pritchard, and William Laurence) advanced explicitly and in detail the alternative theory of natural selection foreshadowed by Erasmus

---

[4] Jacques Barzun, *Darwin, Marx, Wagner*, 2nd ed. (Garden City, NY: Doubleday and Co., 1959), p. 69.

[5] Niles Eldredge, "Progress in Evolution?" *New Scientist*, vol. 110 (June 5, 1986), p. 55.

> Darwin. These three communications were the first clear statements of such an idea — in opposition to notions of evolution guided by design and purpose — since classical times.[6]

Erasmus Darwin was Charles Darwin's grandfather and was a widely read and popular writer on evolution even before Charles was born. Wells, Pritchard, and Laurence were all physicians who wrote on evolution and natural selection almost a half-century before *The Origin of Species*. Diderot in France, Edward Blyth in England, and even Benjamin Franklin advanced similar theories. However, Charles Darwin never acknowledged his predecessors and always called natural selection "my theory."

He was also much influenced by other evolutionary predecessors such as Lamarck, who was most famous for his theory of evolution by acquired characters, and Chambers, who had advocated a form of pantheistic evolution in an influential book called *Vestiges of the Natural History of Creation*. Although Darwin denounced Lamarck's theory, he later superimposed much of it on his own theory.

Darwin was also much influenced by Thomas Malthus and his concept of the "struggle for existence" among human populations. But probably his most important immediate predecessor was Charles Lyell, with his geological dogma of uniformitarianism. The supposed vast span of geologic time was, of course, an absolute necessity for any viable theory of evolution. Darwin frequently acknowledged his debt to Lyell, who was his close friend and advisor, even though he was always reluctant to give credit to his other forerunners. Lyell rejected the predominant catastrophist theory of geology and persuaded his contemporaries that all the geologic strata had been laid down slowly over vast periods of time. Darwin found this framework made to order for his ideas of natural selection, which would certainly require tremendous stretches of time to be effective.

> Darwin and Wallace were Lyell's intellectual children. Both would have failed to be what they were without the *Principles of Geology* to guide them.[7]

With respect to the so-called "evidences for evolution," these had been well expounded long before 1859. Even during the Darwin

---

[6] C. D. Darlington, "The Origin of Darwinism," *Scientific American*, vol. 201 (May 1959), p. 62.

[7] Loren C. Eiseley, "Charles Lyell," *Scientific American*, vol. 201 (August 1959), p. 106.

centennial year, Darlington commented:

> In favor of the evolution of animals from "one living filament," Erasmus Darwin [who died before Charles was born] assembled the evidence of embryology, comparative anatomy, systematics, geographical distribution and, so far as man is concerned, the facts of history and medicine. . . . These arguments about the fact of transformation were all of them already familiar. As to the means of transformation, however, Erasmus Darwin originated almost every important idea that has ever appeared in evolutionary theory.[8]

It does seem strange that Charles Darwin would never acknowledge his intellectual debt to these predecessors, especially his own grandfather, whose books he had certainly read. His admirers speak of him as though he were a paragon of the careful, open-minded scientist — humble, interested solely in the hard-headed observation and understanding of facts. One of these admirers, George Gaylord Simpson, in a review of Darwin's autobiography, commented thus:

> Darwin himself . . . wrote he "never happened to come across a single naturalist who seemed to doubt about the permanence of species," and he acknowledged no debt to his predecessors. These are extraordinary statements. They cannot be literally true, yet Darwin cannot be consciously lying, and he therefore may be judged unconsciously misleading, naive, forgetful, or all three. His own grandfather, Erasmus Darwin, whose work Charles knew very well, was a pioneer evolutionist. Darwin was also familiar with the work of Lamarck, and had certainly met a few naturalists who had flirted with the ideas of evolution. . . . Of all this, Darwin says that none of these forerunners had any effect on him. Then, in almost the next breath, he admits that hearing evolutionary views supported and praised rather early in life may have favored his upholding them later.[9]

Simpson tries to excuse him in the same manner as the writer of

---

[8] C. D. Darlington, "The Origin of Darwinism," p. 61-62.

[9] George G. Simpson, "Charles Darwin in Search of Himself," review of *Autobiography of Charles Darwin*, by Nora Barlow, *Scientific American*, vol. 200 (August 1959), p. 119.

his biography, Nora Barlow, his granddaughter, who said that Darwin had simply dismissed all these predecessors because they did not back up their theories with evidence. Of course, when it comes to real *evidence*, Charles Darwin had none either. He may have found examples in which natural selection was effective in weeding out unfit varieties, but none in which natural selection *produced* new favorable characteristics that could not have resulted from normal variations within the kind.

The most illustrious of Darwin's evolutionist predecessors was probably Jean-Baptiste de Lamarck. He had, of course, proposed as his evolutionary mechanism the inheritance of acquired characteristics, and had written in great depth upon the process and meaning of evolution. Darwin bitterly attacked Lamarck's ideas, yet later he gradually incorporated many of them into his own system, including a modified form of acquired character inheritance.

Darlington said:

> Darwin was slippery . . . [using] a flexible strategy which is not to be reconciled with even average intellectual integrity. . . . He began more and more to grudge praise to those who had in fact paved the way for him. . . . Darwin damned Lamarck and also his grandfather for being very ill-dressed fellows at the same moment he was engaged in stealing their clothes.[10]

There was also Herbert Spencer, whose writings had a profound influence on the acceptance of evolution in the 19th century. It was Spencer who coined the Darwinian phrases "struggle for existence" and "survival of the fittest," and he also was writing on evolution for some time before Darwin began to do so.

> In his own day, which was that of Darwin, too, Spencer was regarded as a giant, and his *Principles of Biology* was adduced as one of the chief evidences for this high estimation. Of course, this could not be on literary grounds. Spencer is no more a first-class stylist than Darwin. . . . Had Darwin and Spencer been more tendentious men, they would doubtless have become embroiled in Newton-Leibniz disputes regarding priorities. . . . It would be difficult to establish the interlocking priorities here. Spencer's preliminary essays were published some

[10] C. D. Darlington, *Darwin's Place in History* (London, 1959), p. 60, 62.

time before *The Origin of Species*.[11]

We should also, of course, mention Thomas Huxley, who was probably more responsible than any other single person for the rapid and widespread acceptance of Darwinian evolution, through his constant and effective speaking and writing. Huxley was an evolutionist before Darwin, but the latter's book gave him the needed scientific support for it, or so he thought. He became known as "Darwin's bulldog." Huxley opposed not only creationism, but Christianity in general, lecturing against the resurrection of Christ and other biblical truths, and applying to himself the term *agnostic*, which he invented. That he was not without ulterior motives in all this is evinced by the fact that Huxley had a driving ambition for fame and historical recognition:

> He had a work to do in England, a messianic purpose, and he dedicated to that purpose his tireless energy and his vast resources of knowledge and ability. And he did attain the success his heart desired, for Huxley was recognized as a prophet in his own country.[12]

Therefore, in no sense could Charles Darwin be said to be responsible for the theory of evolution. The remarkable chain of events leading up to the publication of his book, and the even more remarkable results of its publication, have not even yet been satisfactorily explained. One thing is sure — it was not simply the instant triumph of science over superstition that evolutionary propagandists like to suppose. Darlington says this about Darwin's surprising success:

> He was able to put his ideas across not so much because of his scientific integrity, but because of his opportunism, his equivocation and his lack of historical sense. Though his admirers will not like to believe it, he accomplished his revolution by personal weakness and strategic talent more than by scientific virtue.[13]

These developments, of course, were not taking place in a vacuum. Most scientific writers on the history of evolution write as though the whole story is simply one of the advance of science, and of the delivery of mankind from the cloud of ignorance and superstition that had

---

[11] George Kimball Plochmann, "Darwin or Spencer?" *Science*, vol. 130 (November 27, 1959), p. 1452.

[12] Charles S. Blinderman, "Thomas Henry Huxley," *Scientific Monthly* (April 1957), p. 172.

[13] C. D. Darlington, "The Origin of Darwinism," p. 66.

covered humanity before Darwin. But the middle of the 19th century was a time of great political and social ferment, and scientists as well as others were being caught up in these movements. Europe was still involved in the aftermath of the French Revolution, and other revolutionary movements were seething everywhere. Socialism and Communism were familiar terms, and so was anarchism. These were the times of Hegel and Karl Marx, of the industrial revolution and the American Civil War, of Nietzsche and the growth of economic imperialism.

It has become almost a cliché that "evolution was in the air" and, for that matter, so was "revolution." All the great political and economic movements — whether communism, economic imperialism, centralized capitalism, racism, or others — were all eager to embrace Darwinism as scientific justification for their particular brands of man's basic self-centered struggle-and-survival ethic.

Although faith in the Bible and creation was still very strong in both Europe and America, resulting from the spiritual revivals of the Reformation Period and of the Great Awakening, there had been strong undercurrents of unbelief for a long time. Subversive revolutionary movements were influencing multitudes. Deist philosophers, Unitarian theologians, Illuminist conspirators, Masonic syncretists, and other faith-mongers were all exerting strong influences away from biblical Christianity and back to paganistic pantheism.

The French Revolution had injected its poisons of atheism and immoralism into Europe's bloodstream, and the German rationalistic philosophers had laid the groundwork for the destruction of biblical theology in the schools and churches. Socialism and Communism were on the upswing throughout Europe; Marx and Nietzsche were propagating their deadly theories and were acquiring many disciples — perhaps also financial backers, as students of conspiracies have frequently suggested. All these people and movements were evolutionists of one breed or another.

Significantly, all the above movements and many others of like kind had rejected the biblical cosmology and followed an evolutionary cosmology as their basic rationale. However, there were two strong barriers holding back the tide of paganism. In the first place, the Christian churches and schools had been strengthened by the works of many great Christian apologists (e.g., Paley, Lyttelton, West, Butler, Edwards, Dwight, *et al.*), whose labors had all but demolished the systems of deism and Unitarianism.

In the second place, the Industrial Revolution had drastically increased public awareness and respect for science and technology, and the great scientists of the day were mostly Bible-believing Christians. Scientific philosophy was structured largely around natural theology, and scientific study was considered to be, as the great Isaac Newton had said, "thinking God's thoughts after Him." All the data of natural science were understood as supporting the facts of divine creation and providence; even the sediments and fossils of the new science of geology were understood in terms of the great worldwide Flood.

Sir Isaac Newton is generally acknowledged to have had the greatest scientific intellect of all time, and the weight of his immense authority had long been cited in favor of belief in the full authority of the Bible. He, as did his colleague at Cambridge, John Woodward, believed in the literal creation account of Genesis, as well as that of the worldwide Flood. In fact, Newton was a follower of the eminent scholar Archbishop James Ussher, whose biblical chronology is unjustly ridiculed today by multitudes who exhibit only a small fraction of the ability and careful scholarship that Ussher manifested in his day.

In fact, the period from 1650 to 1880 was an era of scientific giants, and many of the greatest among them — men such as Pascal, Faraday, Maxwell, and Kelvin — were men who believed in the inspiration and authority of the Bible. The marvelous discoveries and achievements of science, revealing the complexities and orderly relationships in nature, seemed more and more to confirm the fact of design and, therefore, the existence of a Creator.[14]

Consequently, if the great complex of anti-Christian movements and philosophies was to be successful in its struggle for control of the minds and hearts of men, something would have to be done first of all to undermine biblical creation and to establish evolution as the accepted cosmogony. The biblical doctrine of origins, of course, is foundational to all other doctrines, and if that could be refuted, or even diluted, then eventually the other doctrines of biblical theology would be undermined and destroyed.

The powerful argument from design in nature, as evidence for God and His creation, would need to be explained by some other means, some naturalistic means, before evolution could really become acceptable to most people. And such a new explanation would need to be a "scientific" explanation, or sufficiently so to convince the scientific community that it would really explain and confirm evolution. If the scientists could be converted to evolution, then the science-honoring public would soon go

[14] See the Henry M. Morris' book *Men of Science, Men of God*, for brief biographies and testimonies of over 100 great Bible-believing scientists of the past (Green Forest, AR: Master Books, 1988).

along, especially in view of man's basic tendency to rebel against God anyhow.

For a while, it seemed that Lamarck's theory of evolution by the inheritance of acquired characters would serve the purpose. The theory had a superficial appearance of plausibility and did seem to provide an alternate explanation for the evidences of design in nature. Lamarck, with his own bitter hatred of the Bible and Christianity, argued his theory very forcefully and persuaded many people of its value. Karl Marx and his colleagues followed Lamarck to some extent, and their successors continued to impose it on Communist biology until recent times.

To most people, however, the idea of the inheritance of acquired characters was so contrary to all experience that they could never really take it seriously, much as they might *like* to believe it. Consequently, a better theory was urgently needed, one that would both commend itself to scientists and also be simple enough for the average man to understand and somehow in keeping with his own common sense experience.

The idea of natural selection in the struggle for existence was the perfect solution! Everyone was familiar with the effectiveness of artificial selection in breeding, so why wouldn't the same process work in nature? Add the factor of the great spans of geologic time conveniently provided by Lyell's uniformitarianism, and everything was present to explain away the evidence of design and even the real necessity of a Creator. Or at least this was the way it would seem, and that was all that was necessary.

The time was, therefore, ripe for the Darwinian theory. As noted above, it really wasn't Darwin's theory, but he was the one who was advocating it at the time when it became propitious to renounce Lamarckianism and to adopt natural selection instead. Huxley, Lyell, and others prodded Darwin to publish his book, which he had been painfully working on for many years, and, when published, it soon became famous. Huxley, along with Spencer, Haeckel, and others, immediately opened a relentless evolutionary propaganda campaign, and it wasn't long until essentially the whole world was converted to evolutionism.

One may sense from the foregoing sequence of events intimations of ominous undercurrents contributing to them. The coincidences seem so improbable, and the results so far-reaching, that one can hardly avoid wondering whether the factors culminating in these developments may not have involved more than mere accidents of history.

Evolutionism before Darwin

One important point must be strongly emphasized, if we are to gain a proper appreciation for the vital importance of special creation to true Christianity and to the modern world in general. Evolution is not a modern scientific discovery or breakthrough of some kind. In the first place, it is not scientific at all (as shown in Volume 2 of this Trilogy), but rather a deadly anti-Christian philosophy and world view. Secondly, it did not originate with Charles Darwin or any other modern scientist or group of scientists.

> Although it is customary to credit the inception of this theory to Charles Darwin and his immediate predecessors, a rudimentary form of this notion can be traced back to the beginnings of written history itself. In fact, the belief that life had its origins in a single basic substance is so widespread among the various peoples of the world, primitive or civilized, that it can be considered one of the few universal themes in the history of ideas.[15]

It is clear that there were many evolutionists before Darwin. In fact, as noted previously, most of the standard present-day textbook "evidences" for evolution were published and well-known long before the *Origin of Species*. However, these views were not predominant, even in the educational world, until the rise of Darwinism. The influence of Christianity had for a long time relegated pagan philosophies to a sort of intellectual underground, and the biblical cosmology was generally accepted in the western world, both by scholars and laymen.

There is no doubt, however, that pagan and gnostic philosophies had exerted some influence on Christian thought, even at the very beginning of church history. These influences are reflected in the frequent uses of allegorical methods of biblical exegesis, attempting to harmonize Scripture with then-current cosmological and philosophical notions, and in the frequent lapse of Christian mystics into a sort of pious pantheism. Both tendencies are often accompanied by evolutionary speculations of various kinds.

> During this period it is significant that several of the church fathers expressed ideas of organic evolution even though the trend of ecclesiastical thought led more readily into other lines of reasoning. St. Gregory of Nyssa (A.D.

[15] Ernest L. Abel, *Ancient Views on the Origin of Life* (Fairleigh Dickinson University Press, 1973), p. 15.

> 331-396), St. Basil (A.D. 331-379), St. Augustine (A.D. 353-430), and St. Thomas Aquinas (A.D. 1225-1274) expressed belief in the symbolical nature of the biblical story of creation and in their comments made statements clearly related to the concept of evolution.[16]

It is true, no doubt, that the dominant point of view in Christendom during these years was in support of literal creation. At the same time, it was not true, as often charged, that the concept of a stationary earth and geocentric universe, as held by many of these writers, originated in the Bible. The Bible teaches neither of these things, but the church of those centuries was also largely dominated by the philosophy of Aristotle, and these ideas were part of his system, as well as that of Ptolemy.

It is also generally recognized that the church of the post-Apostolic period down to the very time of the Reformation was much influenced by gnosticism, and by other forms of Greek philosophy. The Christian scholars of those centuries, exactly as many at the present time, felt that it was essential to work out a compromise cosmology which would be acceptable to the intellectuals of their day. This they did by the simple expedient of interpreting the Scriptures allegorically, which technique, of course, can easily convert meanings into anything that one wishes.

> This desire to find allegories in Scripture was carried to excess by Origen (185-254) who was likewise associated with Alexandrian thought, and he managed thereby to get rid of anything which could not be harmonized with pagan learning, such as the separation of the waters above the firmament from those below it, mentioned in Genesis, which he takes to mean that we should separate our spirits from the darkness of the abyss, where the Adversary and his angels dwell.[17]

As far as the Gnostics themselves were concerned, they were fragmented into many different sects, and it is difficult to generalize about all of them. Most were characterized by an Oriental dualism, and believed in a sharp differentiation between the world of the spirit and the world of matter. The latter was believed to be eternal, rather than specially created by God, and this, of course, is the main pillar of an evolutionary system. The personal incarnation and bodily resurrection

[16] Arthur Ward Lindsey, *Principles of Organic Evolution* (St. Louis, MO: The C. V. Mosby Co., 1962), p. 21.

[17] J. L. E. Dreyer, "Medieval Cosmology," *Theories of the Universe*, ed. Milton K. Munitz (Glencoe, IL: The Free Press, 1957), p. 117.

of Christ were denied, as well as many of the other central doctrines of Christianity.

For the most part, however, as noted, Christians both in the dominant state churches and in the various smaller groups outside these churches retained their faith in the biblical view of creation. This conviction was especially strengthened by the great increase in Bible circulation following the Reformation and later spiritual awakenings.

As a minority belief, however, evolution was not uncommon. Spontaneous generation had been accepted as common knowledge at least since the time of Aristotle, and was opposed only by a minority of Christians who recognized it as unscriptural. Ideas of transmutation were also widely held, even in the realm of inorganic materials, as evinced by the studies of the alchemists.

Two levels of evolutionary beliefs need to be recognized. At the intellectual level, Greek atomistic philosophies, such as those worked out by Democritus and Leucippus, were highly developed and were accepted by many scholars. The pagan mystery religions were understood and practiced by initiates on a considerably higher plan of sophistication than the popular idol worship of the masses. The Stoic and Epicurean philosophers, the best known of whom is probably Lucretius, were essentially either atheists or evolutionary pantheists. None of the pagan religions or philosophies held any real belief in a personal, omnipotent, eternal Creator, who created all things *ex nihilo* by His omnipotent Word.

The philosophy of Aristotle, who did teach a quasi-creation doctrine while simultaneously advocating spontaneous generation and the eternal pre-existence of the universe, the philosophy of the Stoics, and the various gnostic philosophies, all had significant influence in keeping the pagan cosmologies alive even in the Christian churches. With the Renaissance came a great humanistic revival of pagan philosophies, and these came to real fruit in the full-blown evolutionary cosmologies of Kant and LaPlace, with their nebular hypotheses, of Descartes, with his mechanistic philosophy, of Spinoza and others.

On the popular level, however, the philosophical pantheism of the ancient scholars was expressed in the pantheon of gods and goddesses associated with the pagan religions. When these were finally replaced by Christianity, they went underground, as it were. To some extent, the idols were "baptized" with Christian names, and the old polytheistic nature-worship was incorporated into the customs and practices of the churches. At the same time, the demonic and occultic aspects of paganism were perpetuated in various forms of witchcraft, which continued to thrive throughout the Middle Ages and even into modern times.

All of these systems — philosophical pantheism, popular polytheism, and occult supernaturalism — are fundamentally evolutionary world views. All were and are bitter opponents of biblical Christianity, rejecting any concept of a personal God, who created all things, including the physical universe itself, by special creation *ex nihilo.* It is from such as these that the modern theory of evolution must trace its ancestry. Diverse though the "gods many" (1 Cor. 8:5) may be in detail, they are all one in their hatred for the true God of creation.

Evolutionism in the Pre-Christian World

The most influential of the Greek philosophers was Aristotle (384-322 B.C.). He, of course, was a student of Plato (427-348 B.C.), and Plato of Socrates (470-399 B.C.). It has been argued whether these men were evolutionists or creationists, and there is no doubt that they did believe in God, as a First Cause, or prime mover. Their cosmogonies are not very specific in detail. However, it is well known that Aristotle believed in spontaneous generation, and that is certainly a form of evolution. Furthermore, he believed in the concept that the world never had a beginning, which doctrine, of course, is totally inconsistent with true creationism.

> Like his master Plato, Aristotle insists there is but one world, that is a central body like the earth surrounded by a finite number of planets and stars. This one world, of course, which makes up the entire universe, contains all existent matter. . . . Aristotle argues that the one world or universe we know is eternal, without beginning and without end.[18]

Even earlier than these philosophers, however, a much more consistently pantheistic and evolutionary view of the universe was widely believed, and continued to exercise profound influence on all subsequent scientific thought even into modern times. This was the "atomistic" school.

> The type of thinking initiated by the Milesian school of pre-Socratic thinkers — Thales, Anaximander, and Anaximenes — in the sixth century B.C. was carried forward in many directions. One of the most remarkable

---

[18] Milton K. Munitz, ed., *Theories of the Universe* (Glencoe, IL: The Free Press, 1957), p. 63-64. Munitz was Professor of Philosophy at New York University.

> outcomes of such speculations, representing a culmination of their materialistic thought, was to be found in the atomist school. Originally worked out in its main features by Leucippus and Democritus in the fifth century B.C., the teachings of atomism were later adopted as a basis for the primarily ethical philosophy of Epicureanism. . . . It elaborates the conception of a universe whose order arises out of a blind interplay of atoms rather than as a product of deliberate design; of a universe boundless in spatial extent, infinite in its duration and containing innumerable worlds in various stages of development or decay. . . . It was the same conception, however, which once more came into the foreground of attention at the dawn of modern thought and has remained up to the present time an inspiration for those modes of scientific thinking that renounce any appeal to teleology in the interpretation of physical phenomena.[19]

Modern evolutionary materialists are not so modern after all. Their system is essentially the same as the pre-Socratic Greek cosmology of 2,500 years ago! The system continued through the Roman period, with one of its leading exponents being the Roman poet Lucretius. A typical excerpt from his philosophical writings follows:

> Certainly the atoms did not post themselves purposefully in due order by an act of intelligence, nor did they stipulate what movements each should perform. As they have been rushing everlastingly throughout all space in their myriads, undergoing myriad changes under the disturbing impact of collisions, they have experienced every variety of movement and conjunction till they have fallen into the particular pattern by which this world of ours is constituted. This world has persisted many a long year, having once been set going in the appropriate motions. From these everything else follows.[20]

The still earlier Greek philosophers, beginning apparently with Thales (640-546 B.C.), were also evolutionists and materialists. Thales' home was Miletus, and his followers are called the Milesian school, and also the Ionian school.

---

[19] Milton K. Munitz, ed., *Theories of the Universe* (Glencoe, IL: The Free Press, 1957), p. 6.

[20] Lucretius, *The Nature of the Universe,* trans. R. E. Latham, (New York, NY: Penguin Books, 1951), p. 58. Lucretius lived from 96 to 55 B.C.

> The Milesian system pushed back to the very beginning of things the operation of processes as familiar and ordinary as a shower of rain. It made the formation of the world no longer a supernatural, but a natural event. Thanks to the Ionians, and to no one else, this has become the universal premise of all modern science.[21]

That concept of evolutionary development is not, of course, exactly that of modern Darwinism, but the essentials are there:

> The order arose by differentiation out of a simple state of things, at first conceived as a single living substance, later by the pluralists, as a primitive confusion in which "all things," now separate, "were together."[22]

Thales was influenced in his thinking especially by the Egyptians and the Phoenicians, as well as by the cosmogonic myths of the Greeks themselves, particularly as recorded by Hesiod. The scope of this study does not warrant a detailed tracing of the cosmogonies of all the ancient peoples — Persians, Syrians, Egyptians, Canaanites, and others. If that were done, however, it could be shown that all of them, in one way or another, were essentially evolutionists, with the one exception, of course, of the Hebrews. As one illustration, however, let us consider another great nation, in a completely different part of the world, also with a long history — namely, China.

> In contrast to the Western world, the Far Eastern philosophers thought of creation in evolutionary terms. . . . The striking feature of the Chinese concept of cosmogony is the fact that creation was never associated with the design or activity of a supernatural being, but rather with the interaction of impersonal forces, the powers of which persist interminably.[23]

Some of the Chinese speculations, in fact, go into amazing detail concerning the supposed sequences of organic evolution, proceeding organism by organism from the simplest plants upward through grubs, insects, birds, leopards, horses, and men:

---

[21] F. M. Cornford, "Pattern of Ionian Cosmogony" in *Theories of the Universe*, ed. Milton K. Munitz, p. 21.

[22] *Ibid.*, p. 22.

[23] Ilza Veith, "Creation and Evolution in the Far East," in *Issues in Evolution*, ed. Sol Tax (Chicago, IL: University of Chicago Press, 1960), p. 1-2.

> Though completely fanciful, this ladder of nature is noteworthy because it was conceived more than two millennia before the Western world began to re-examine its biblical chronology. But beyond this, the above-quoted passage contains two highly important points: first, a belief in an inherent continuity of all creation and, second, a reference to the merging of one species into another — from primordial germ to man.[24]

However, it is also significant that the very *oldest* Chinese traditions seem to focus on a high God who created all things. This belief was superseded early by the above evolutionary speculations, and eventually by the sophisticated pantheism of Taoism, Confucianism, and Buddhism.

The ancient cosmogonies of India also are evolutionary. All of these systems regard the earth as extremely old, perhaps infinite in age. Those modern writers who like to boast of the "discovery" that the earth is billions of years old instead of thousands, as a great achievement of modern science seem to be ignorant of the almost universal belief of the ancients in evolution and the great antiquity of the earth.

In the light of these facts, the common charge that Moses wrote Genesis in terms of special creation, rather than in those of the more sophisticated concept of evolution, as an accommodation to the naive culture of the Hebrews to whom he was writing, is itself obviously inexcusably naive! The only cosmogonies that Moses' people could have encountered in the world of their day, apart from Genesis, were evolutionary cosmogonies. The concept of a special, recent creation of all things was a radical, new concept, and would have had to be plainly and definitely set forth in the clearest terms in order for them to grasp it!

Not only do evolutionary systems appear among all the ancient philosophies and religions, however. In spite of many differences in detail, it is well-known that the very religions themselves are all essentially the same. Whether in Greece, Rome, Egypt, Canaan, India, or anywhere else, the basic systems prove to be equivalent to each other. Each involves an array of gods and goddesses representing various aspects of nature and life, altogether comprising the great world-spirit which is essentially the personification of the universe itself. The gods and goddesses in each nation usually have exact counterparts in the pantheons of other nations, and the ritualistic systems, especially the "mysteries"

---

[24] Ilza Veith, "Creation and Evolution in the Far East," in *Issues in Evolution*, ed. Sol Tax (Chicago, IL: University of Chicago Press, 1960), p. 7.

imparted to their respective initiates, are likewise equivalent.

The modern notion is that these pagan gods and goddesses were simply imaginary creatures in naive myths and fairy tales. The fact is, however, that ancient people — as well as modern pagan worshippers, including animists — were far more sophisticated in their approach to the understanding of nature than we realize. As Abel says,

> In general, myth conveys the impression of a story invented *ex nihilo*, a story describing the irascible and typically irresponsible actions of various divine malcontents. But these deities are not simply malevolent gods capriciously toying with mankind. They are actually personifications of Nature, and their activities, predictable and unpredictable, determine what life will be like on earth.[25]

It is these assorted deities — personifying the sea, land, fire, feelings, loves and hatreds, and all the other various systems and forces of nature (which in turn are personified as the great Mother) — who produce and control plants and animals and people and their destinies. This polytheism is thus merely the popular face on the evolutionary pantheism that constitutes the common heritage of all nations, with the exception of those few who still believed in monotheism and the one personal God of all creation. Furthermore, their commonality — the same deities and activities, though with different names corresponding to their different languages — surely indicates that they all were derived originally from a common source.

The classic work of Alexander Hislop, *The Two Babylons*, has never been answered. In this work Hislop documents from an abundance of sources the primeval unity of the various pagan religions and traces their origin back to the first Babylon. He says:

> These mysteries were long shrouded in darkness, but now the thick darkness begins to pass away. All who have paid the least attention to the literature of Greece, Egypt, Phoenicia, or Rome are aware of the place which the "Mysteries" occupy in these countries, and that, whatever circumstantial diversities there might be, in all essential respects these "Mysteries" in the different countries were the same. Now, as the language of Jeremiah (51:7) would indicate that Babylon was the primal source from which all

[25] Abel, *Ancient Views on Origin*, p. 15.

> these systems of idolatry flowed, so the deductions of the most learned historians, on more historical grounds, have led to the same conclusion.[26]

One need not agree with Hislop's argument that this ancient Babylonian system is now represented essentially by Roman Catholicism to appreciate his strong case that the various pagan religions had a common source in Babylon — or better, in the original Babel.

In any case, it is evident that the Babylonian cosmogony must be very ancient, and must have had profound influence on those of other ancient nations. In modern times, it has been rediscovered by archaeologists, and is known as *Enuma Elish*.[27] In the form now available, it is believed to have been written about 2600 B.C., and thus to have been written before Moses' time. Many people, therefore, have erroneously concluded that Moses borrowed his creation account from this source, but the truth is that the *Enuma Elish* represents at best a corrupted form of the true record that was handed down to Moses by the early patriarchs.

Actually, *Enuma Elish* is the Babylonian cosmogonical myth, and like all the others, it is an evolutionary system. From such as these the later philosophers, like Thales, sought to extract the "true" materialistic history of the earth.

> One evidence of the influence of myth upon these earliest instances of "scientific" thought is to be found in the interest in formulating a complete cosmogony which would show how from some primordial state an ordered world arose and underwent successive differentiations of an astronomic, geographic, and meteorologic kind, culminating ultimately, in the mergence of living things and human society.[28]

All such myths began with matter in some form already in existence, and then the forces of nature (or the gods who personify those natural forces) are described as operating upon this primeval matter in such ways as to bring a cosmos out of the chaos. The early philosophers then placed the popular polytheism in a scientific framework, proposing

---

[26] Alexander Hislop, *The Two Babylons,* Amer. ed. (New York, NY: Loizeaux Brothers, 1950), p. 12. This book was originally published in Edinburgh in 1858 and has gone through numerous editions and printings.

[27] Alexander Heidel, *The Babylonian Genesis* (Chicago, IL: University of Chicago Press, 1959).

[28] Milton K. Munitz, *Space, Time, and Creation* (Glencoe, IL: The Free Press, 1957), p. 8–9.

the development of things from some primordial stuff, such as fire or atoms, or, most commonly, water.

Specifically, *Enuma Elish* assumes that all things have evolved out of water.

> This description presents the earliest stage of the universe as one of watery chaos. The chaos consisted of three intermingled elements: Apsu, who represents the sweet waters; Ti'amat, who represents the sea; and Mumsu, who cannot as yet be identified with certainty but may represent cloud banks and mist. These three types of water were mingled in a large undefined mass. . . . Then, in the midst of this watery chaos, two gods came into existence — Lahau and Lahamu.[29]

Then the epic goes on to describe how other gods were generated and then engaged in various activities, including fighting and killing one another. Eventually the god Marduk gained control of the heavenly host and thence proceeded to the formation of the earth and stars and man, the latter actually from the blood of one of the slain gods.

The complicated battles of the gods and goddesses seem to portray the struggling forces of nature as they labor to bring forth an orderly world. Or, perhaps, they may rather represent actual warfare in the heavens, such as the Bible describes, between Satan and his angels and Michael and his angels. Or possibly both.

In any case, such tales are certainly infinitely inferior to the true record of creation as given in the first chapter of Genesis. The idea that Genesis could have been derived from such mythology as this is incredible.

We have thus shown that the evolutionary philosophy is not modern at all, but, rather, traces back through all the history of mankind, right back to Babylon — not the Babylon of Nebuchadnezzar (though it was prominent there), but to the original Babel founded by Nimrod (Gen. 10:8-10). Furthermore, the evolutionary system is foundational to the system of pantheistic polytheism which constituted the universal religion of the ancients, and which also was derived from Babel.

Moreover, this system invariably is identified in some way with astrology, and all the various divinities are associated with their own particular stars or planets. To the pagans, these heavenly beings were not considered as mere religious ideals, but as living spirits, capable of

---

[29] Thorkild Jacobsen, "Enuma Elish—the Babylonian Genesis," in *Theories of the Universe,* ed. Milton K. Munitz, p. 9.

communicating directly with men through oracles or seers or mediums. Pantheism, polytheism, astrology, idolatry, mysteries, spiritism, materialism — this whole great complex of belief and practice, superficially diverse, but fundamentally one — constitutes the gigantic rebellion of mankind against the true God of creation. Always, whatever the outward appearance, the underlying faith is in eternal matter, in a self-contained cosmos evolving upward out of chaos toward future perfection.

Though in some cases, particularly isolated tribes, the people seem to have retained some kind of dim awareness of a great high God, far removed in time and space from their personal lives, their practical interests have from primeval times almost invariably been centered in the multiple divinities connected with their own immediate environments. Such identification of ultimate reality with finite natural objects is nothing but evolution. Matter in some form, not God, is their original and eternal cause of all things.

The connection of the pantheon of gods and goddesses with the stars, planets, and constellations in the system known as astrology is significant. Astrology, with its signs of the Zodiac, seems to have been the common heritage of all nations and their ancient religious systems. It is also prominent in the modern "New Age" revival of ancient pantheism. The stars were believed to be essentially identical with the various deities that they represented (Mars, Venus, etc.) and thus to exert much control over human lives. Abel expressed this as follows:

> For instance, when the Babylonian priests turned their attention to natural phenomena such as the stars, it was for the purpose of knowing better the will of the gods whose actions were believed to be intimately linked with the movements of these heavenly bodies.[30]

In common with all other features of paganism, whether ancient or modern, astrology is an evolutionary system, rejecting the concept of the transcendent God who created the stars, as well as the fallen angels (who came eventually to be worshipped as deities) who presumably inhabit their respective stars and planets. All of these, as well as all other beings and systems, were believed to have evolved out of the primeval waters. This belief seems to have originated in Babel (though it was also prominent in ancient Egypt) and eventually was incorporated by Thales and his Milesian followers into the Greek cosmology.

> In the end, observation and introspection caused him

[30] Abel, *Ancient Views on Origin*, p. 23.

(Thales) to conclude that all the variations in Nature could in fact be accounted for in terms of a single substance — water.[31]

In view of the apparently common origin of all ancient religions, it also seems significant that most of their cosmogonies begin with the world already in existence, but consisting primarily of pervasive waters everywhere. The significant point is that the Genesis cosmogony, on the other hand, does *not* begin with water, but with God. Then the first act of creation by God was to speak the space/mass/time universe into being — not in completed form (*that* was done in six days, as a pattern for man's future work week), but in a form that initially *did* consist primarily of pervasive waters.

This fascinating situation provides the clue from which we may be able finally to trace out the ultimate source of the great global age-long deception of evolution.

The Ultimate Origin of Evolutionism

The origin of evolution as a religious philosophy (and that, of course, is all that it can ever be) is thus locked together with the origin of paganism, which in the post-diluvian world was undoubtedly at Babel. This origin is also intimated by Scripture, when it speaks of "Mystery, Babylon the Great, the mother of harlots and abominations of the earth" (Rev. 17:5). Since Nimrod was the founder and first ruler of Babylon, it seems reasonable to propose that he was responsible for the introduction of this entire religious system into the life of mankind.

To the modern skeptic, of course, Nimrod is merely a nonexistent legendary hero like all the other names recorded in the early chapters of Genesis. Such skeptics should at least realize, however, that the literature of antiquity frequently refers to Nimrod in one way or another. There were many people in ancient times, in addition to the writer of Genesis, who regarded him as real.

Numerous ancient historians recognize Nimrod and his exploits, and various sites in the Babylonian-Nineveh region are associated by the Arabs with his name. It is quite possible that the chief god of the Babylonians (Marduk, or Merodach) really represents the same Nimrod, deified after his death.

Obviously, however, when we attempt to decipher history of this degree of antiquity, we have little to go on. This is the period in which fact and legend are almost indistinguishable. Although a great deal of archaeological excavation has been done in the Tigris-Euphrates

[31] *Ibid.*, p. 24.

valleys, the monuments are difficult to translate, and only a small fraction even of the recovered materials has really been read. Much still remains to be excavated, and, of course, the far greater part has long since been destroyed by the ravages of time.

We do, of course, have the record of Genesis 10 and 11. Though these chapters are tantalizingly brief, we can have confidence that the information they give is true. To the skeptic, we can say at least two things — no one has disproved the validity of these verses, and he has as yet nothing better to offer.

In this section, as we seek to understand the ultimate source of the evolutionary system, speculation is admittedly necessary. But at least it is speculation guided by the information given in Scripture, as well as by the historical data that we have been accumulating.

We assume, therefore, that the Babylonian mysteries were originally established by Nimrod and his followers at Babel. They have somehow since been transmitted throughout the world and down through the centuries, corrupting all nations with their materialistic glorification of the "host of heaven," changing the "glory of the uncorruptible God into an image made like to corruptible man, and to birds, and fourfooted beasts, and creeping things" (Rom. 1:23). Because they "did not like to retain God in their knowledge" (Rom. 1:28), they proceeded to change "the truth of God into a lie, and worshipped and served the creature more than the Creator" (Rom. 1:25).

The remarkable similarities and antiquities of the zodiacal constellations and the astrological systems that have come down from all the early nations, provide strong evidence of the primeval unity of heathendom. It therefore is a reasonable deduction, even though hardly capable of proof, that the entire monstrous complex was revealed to Nimrod at Babel by demonic influences, perhaps by Satan himself.

It is significant that the phrase "the host of heaven" is applied in Scripture both to the stars and to angels. Similarly, the worship of the sun, moon, and stars, as well as the mythological deities, and the graven images that represent them, is also frequently identified in Scripture with the worship of angels, and especially with the fallen angels and the demonic hosts who are following Lucifer (Isa. 14:12-14; Rev. 12:4) in his attempt to replace God as king of the universe.

In common with all the other great temple-towers of antiquity, it is likely that the original Tower of Babel (Gen. 11:4) was built, not to "reach unto heaven" in a literal sense (Nimrod was no naive character in a fairy tale to attempt such a project as that) but rather with a "top unto heaven" (the words "may reach" are not in the original). That is, its top was probably a great temple shrine, emblazoned with the zodiacal signs representing the host of heaven, Satan and his "principalities [and] powers, rulers of the darkness of this world" (Eph. 6:12).

These evil spirits perhaps met with Nimrod and his priests there, to plan their long-range strategy against God and His redemptive purposes for the post-deluge world. This included especially the development of a non-theistic cosmology, one which could explain the origin and meaning of the universe and man without acknowledging the true God of creation. Denial of God's power and sovereignty in creation is, of course, foundational in the rejection of His authority in every other sphere.

The solid evidence for the above sequence of events is admittedly tenuous.[32] As a hypothesis, however, it does harmonize with the biblical record and with the known facts of the history of religions, whereas it is difficult to suggest any other hypothesis that does.

If something like this really happened, early in post-diluvian history, then Satan himself is the originator of the concept of evolution. In fact, the Bible does say that he is the one "which deceiveth the whole world" (Rev. 12:9) and that he "hath blinded the minds of them which believe not" (2 Cor. 4:4). Such statements as these must apply especially to the evolutionary cosmology, which indeed is the world view with which the whole world has been deceived.

One question remains. Assuming Satan to be the real source of the evolutionary concept, how did it originate in his mind? He originally was "full of wisdom, and perfect in beauty . . . in the day that thou wast created" (Ezek. 28:12-13). Surely, he knew very well that he, as well as all other angels and everything else, had been created by God, not evolved by natural processes. Knowing this, he could never have the slightest hope of succeeding in the cosmic rebellion that he has been promoting for so many millennia.

A possible answer to this mystery may be that Satan, the father of lies, has not only deceived the whole world and the angelic hosts who followed him, but that he has even deceived himself! The only way he could really *know* about creation (just as the only way *we* can know about creation) was for God to tell him! But "thine heart was lifted up because of thy beauty, thou hast corrupted thy wisdom by reason of thy brightness" (Ezek. 28:17).

The sin of pride and unbelief, the twin source of all other sins,

[32] The sequence of historical events outlined in this chapter has been discussed and documented more thoroughly in the book, *The Long War Against God* by Henry M. Morris (Grand Rapids: Baker Book House, 1989).

resulted in "the condemnation of the devil" (1 Tim. 3:6). Satan refused to believe and accept the Word of God concerning his own creation and place in God's economy. Perhaps resentment at the creation of man in God's image, with the marvelous ability to multiply his own kind (which angels cannot do) and the commissioning of man as God's vice-regent over the earth (infinitely more beautiful and complex than all the stars of heaven) contributed to the nurturing of this unbelieving pride in Satan. He therefore deceived himself into supposing that all things, including himself and including God, had been evolved by natural processes out of the primordial stuff of the universe, and that therefore he himself might hope to become God.

The only evidence he had for creation was God's Word, even though that was eminently reasonable. His first conscious awareness after God created all the angels, evidently on day one of creation week (note Ps. 104:1-5) prior to laying "the foundations of the earth" on day three, was that of the primeval waters (Gen. 1:2). His only alternative to believing that God is eternal and Creator of all things was to assume that both God and the angels also had "evolved" out of the waters! God may have appeared before him, but they were of the same essence, and therefore equal.

Satan therefore said in his self-delulsion, "I will be like the most High" (Isa. 14:14) and God "cast [him] to the ground [same word as 'earth']" (Ezek. 28:17). He then brought about man's fall with the same deception ("ye shall be as gods" — Gen. 3:5), and the long tragic history of the outworking of human unbelief as centered in the grand satanic delusion of evolution has been the result.

Chapter 3

The Corrupt Fruits of Evolutionism

It is not surprising that a world view which denies God and His Word and which is utterly devoid of scientific truth or value should generate ungodly behavior by its followers. Volume 1 of this Trilogy has demonstrated that evolution is completely contrary to the Bible and to the Christian faith, and Volume 2 has documented its unscientific character. Then the first two chapters of this third volume have shown the amazing fact that, despite its unscientific and anti-biblical nature, evolutionism has come to dominate every academic discipline in the schools of the world and that, indeed, it has done so throughout most of human history, in one form or another.

In the remaining chapters of this book, we want to show that practically all the harmful practices and deadly philosophies that plague mankind have their roots and pseudo-rationale in evolutionism. A good way to start is with the ancient pagan notion of the "Great Chain of Being," and its 19th-century stepchild, the evolutionists' famous "recapitulation theory."

The Tragic Heritage of the Recapitulation Theory

The origin of the "Great Chain of Being" concept is lost in antiquity, but Plato discussed it, as did Plotinus and other neo-Platonist philosophers. It had significant impact on the medieval church and was prominent in the writings of many Renaissance scientists and philosophers. The essential idea was that emanations of the cosmos had produced an unbroken chain of entities in the universe, proceeding from the cosmic source of all being, down through spirit beings, to human beings (higher races to lower), to animals (again higher to lower), to plants, to non-organic systems, to basic elements. Even though many links in the unbroken chain are still unknown, they must exist somewhere, so the concept goes.

This notion that there was a continuous chain from complex to simple, or from simple to complex, was also applied by early scientists. They assumed that there must be a continuous chain of structural forms in the animal world, as well as a continuous chain of forms of life developing over the ages. This theory led to the "science" of comparative morphology, in the first case, and to the assumed increasing complexity of fossil forms in the geologic column (an assumption made many years before any significant numbers of fossils had actually been excavated) in the second case. Both systems (similarities of anatomy and the fossil record) were then appropriated by early evolutionists (well before Charles Darwin's time) as evidence of evolution. Of course, as discussed in Volume 2 of the Trilogy, the actual *data* on which both systems were based provide much better evidence of creation. The *gaps* in both cases are far more significant than the similarities and continuities.

A third application of the "Great Chain," as developed especially by German and French naturalists in the century before Darwin, was the assumption that the development of each animal or human embryo in the womb also proceeded from simple to complex through a continuous chain. It was easy, then, for the pre-Darwin evolutionists to associate this development with the assumed development of different forms of life during the geological ages, making the one analogous to and mutually supportive of the other.

Ideas have consequences, and false ideas usually generate bitter consequences. One of the premier examples of this principle thus became the infamous "recapitulation theory," developed by such philosophers as Goethe and Robert Chambers, and then popularized in Darwin's day by Ernst Haeckel, the German atheist. Called by Haeckel the "biogenetic law," this idea was spread widely by his euphonious slogan, "ontogeny recapitulates phylogeny," meaning that embryonic growth of the fetus in the womb rapidly recapitulates (repeats) the entire evolutionary history of the species. This bizarre notion has been cited by credulous evolutionists for over 150 years as one of the main "proofs" of evolution. Darwin, himself, made great use of it in his *Origin of Species* and *Descent of Man*.

Nevertheless, recapitulationism is completely false, and most competent evolutionists today know this. Two leading neo-Darwinists have admitted the error thus:

> Haeckel misstated the evolutionary principle involved. It is now firmly established that ontogeny does *not* repeat phylogeny.[1]

More recently, Dr. Keith Thompson, professor of biology at Yale, said:

> Surely the biogenetic law is as dead as a doornail. It was finally exorcised from biology textbooks in the fifties. As a topic of serious theoretical inquiry, it was extinct in the twenties.[2]

In spite of its specious character, this notion captivated the minds of evolutionists, is still believed by millions of their followers even today, and still finds its way into high school textbooks. Four of the very important, but very bitter fruits produced by the corrupt tree of recapitulationism are discussed briefly below.

1. The Standard Geologic Column

The fossil record has long been considered the definitive evidence of evolution, with simple life forms supposedly preserved in ancient rocks, and complex forms presumably in younger rocks. The dating of the rocks, however, is based on the fossils they contain — not on their vertical position in the sedimentary sequences. Leading evolutionists acknowledge this to be circular reasoning.

> The charge that the construction of the geologic column involves circularity has a certain amount of validity.[3]

> And this poses something of a problem: If we date the rocks by their fossils, how can we then turn around and talk about patterns of evolutionary change through time in the fossil record?[4]

Thus, the key "proof" of evolution is based on the *assumption* of evolution. In fact, pre-Darwinian theistic evolutionists and progressive

---

1 G. G. Simpson and W. Beck, *An Introduction to Biology* (New York, NY: Harcourt Brace and World, 1965), p. 241.

2 Keith S. Thompson, "Ontogeny and Phylogeny Recapitulated," *American Scientist*, vol. 76 (May/June, 1988), p. 273.

3 David M. Raup, "Geology and Creation," *Bulletin of the Field Museum of Natural History*, vol. 54 (March 1983), p. 21.

4 Niles Eldredge, *Time Frames: The Rethinking of Darwinian Evolution and the Theory of Punctuated Equilibrium* (New York, NY: Simon and Schuster, 1985), p. 52.

creationists had already worked out the desired order of the fossils before any significant number of them had even been discovered, so that the geologic column was essentially ready-made as an evidence for evolution when Darwin proposed his theory. They had assumed that there was an innate principle operating in the cosmos and in living organisms that impelled them to proceed upward in complexity, and that this evolutionary order must be the same everywhere — in embryology, morphology, paleontology, and even psychology. It was natural, therefore, for these theorists to use embryological studies as a basis for assigning order to the fossils.

> In Down's day, the theory of recapitulation embodied a biologist's best guide for the organization of life into sequences of higher and lower forms.[5]

> Another major factor keeping some sort of recapitulation alive was the need of comparative morphologists and especially paleontologists for a solid theoretical foundation for homology. They had long since come to rely on comparative ontogenetic information as a base.[6]

Although a number of other factors contributed significantly to the development of the standard stratigraphical column (e.g., the rock sequences in western Europe), embryological studies were perhaps most important of all. This standard geological column is found only in textbooks, however, and all the supposed transitional forms are still missing in the rocks themselves.

2. Freudian Psychoanalysis

Another deadly fruit of the recapitulation idea was the psychological system developed by Sigmund Freud. Although much of his system is now rejected by modern psychologists and psychiatrists, there is no question that all of them (including many Christians) have been profoundly influenced by Darwinism and the whole concept of man's presumed animal ancestry. Recent discovery of a hitherto unpublished manuscript of Freud reveals how strongly he relied on recapitulationism.

> In a 1915 paper Freud demonstrates his preoccupation with evolution. Immersed in the theories of Darwin, and of Lamarck, who believed acquired traits could be

[5] Stephen J. Gould, "Dr. Down's Syndrome," *Natural History,* vol. 89 (April 1980), p. 144.

[6] Thompson, "Ontogeny and Phylogeny Recapitulated," p. 274.

> inherited, Freud concluded that mental disorders were the vestiges of behavior that had been appropriate in earlier stages of evolution.[7]
>
> The evolutionary idea that Freud relied on most heavily in the manuscript is the maxim that "ontogeny recapitulates phylogeny," that is, that the development of the individual recapitulates the evolution of the entire species.[8]

All the anti-Christian impact of Freud's atheistic psychological system, leading even to the modern sexual revolution, so-called, can thus be traced largely back to this recapitulation notion.

3. Modern Racism

Feelings of tribalism, nationalism, and racism have existed ever since Babel, but racism did not reach its most intense and virulent level until it received a pseudo-scientific sanction from Darwinism. This new form of evolutionism, popularized in western Europe and America during the 19th century, with its emphasis on "survival of the fittest," lent itself naturally to the idea of competition between races, with the supposedly more highly evolved races eliminating the "savage races," as Darwin called them,[9] in the "struggle for existence."

Social Darwinism, with its imperialist and racist emphases, became exceedingly strong in the 19th and early 20th centuries, and, even though it went into partial eclipse after World War II, its tragic aftereffects are with us still. Racism reached its zenith under Hitler in Nazi Germany, and the "biogenetic law" of Ernst Haeckel was largely responsible.

> Recapitulation was Haeckel's favorite argument . . . Haeckel and his colleagues also invoked recapitulation to affirm the racial superiority of northern European whites. . . . Herbert Spencer wrote that "the intellectual traits of the uncivilized . . . are traits recurring in the children of the civilized." Carl Vogt said it more strongly in 1864: "The grown up Negro partakes, as regards his intellectual faculties, of the nature of the child. . . ."[10]

---

[7] Daniel Goleman, "Lost Paper Shows Freud's Effort to Link Analysis and Evolution," *New York Times* (February 10, 1987), p. 19.

[8] *Ibid.*, p. 22.

[9] Charles Darwin, *The Descent of Man,* 2nd ed. (New York, NY: A. L. Burt, Co., 1974), p. 178.

[10] Stephen Jay Gould, "Racism and Recapitulation," chap. 27 in *Ever Since Darwin* (New York, NY: W. W. Norton and Co., 1977), p. 217.

> [Haeckel] became one of Germany's major ideologists for racism, nationalism, and imperialism.[11]

> In essence, Haeckel and his fellow social Darwinists advanced the ideas that were to become the core assumptions of national socialism.[12]

Lest anyone misunderstand, although all the above authorities are evolutionists, they do not believe in either recapitulationism or racism. The quotations are brief, but they do not misrepresent their authors. Much more documentation to the same effect could be provided if necessary.

4. The Plague of Abortionism

The most recent application of the recapitulation theory has been as a pseudo-scientific justification for the terrible holocaust of abortionism that has been sweeping the world in recent years. Although there may be many personal reasons that women have abortions and that doctors perform them, the only *scientific* or *religious* justification that can be given for abortion is that the fetus is not yet really a human being. If the embryo is truly human, with human life and an eternal soul, then abortion is obviously cruel, premeditated murder! Therefore, abortionists must deny that the fetus is human. How much easier to destroy an embryo while it is still in a fish stage, or a reptile stage, than to acknowledge it as fully human right from the start.

But the only quasi-scientific rationale for such a pronouncement must be based on recapitulationism. As a widely syndicated columnist says, referring to an article by evolutionary feminist Ellen Goodman:

> I think that what she imagines is that the human embryo undergoes something like the whole process of evolution, as in the old adage that "ontogeny recapitulates phylogeny."[13]

This type of reasoning, of course, is specious, at best, and so is that which justifies racism, or Freudianism, or even the standard evolutionary interpretation of the fossil record. As we have shown, all these

---

[11] Daniel Gasman, *The Scientific Origins of National Socialism: Social Darwinism in Ernst Haeckel and the German Monist League* (New York, NY: American Elsevier, 1971), p. xvii.

[12] George J. Stein, "Biological Science and the Roots of Nazism," *American Scientist*, vol. 76 (January/February 1988), p. 56.

[13] Joseph Sobran, "The Averted Gaze: Liberalism and Fetal Pain," *Human Life Review* (Spring 1984), p. 6.

concepts have been largely based on the discredited quasi-scientific notion of the 19th century that "ontogeny recapitulates phylogeny." There are still other erroneous and harmful ideas that have sprouted from recapitulationism. For example, much of modern criminology has developed out of this same recapitulationist concept.

> A whole school of "criminal anthropology" . . . branded white wrong-doers as genetically retarded. . . . Born criminals are not simply deranged or diseased; they are, literally throwbacks to a previous evolutionary stage.[14]

The summary above gives some insight into the devastating social effects of evolutionism in general and the recapitulation theory in particular. We need not discuss the geological column further here, since this subject is treated at some length in Volume 2.

The subject of racism is treated more fully in chapter 4 of this book, along with its connections with Nazism, social Darwinism, and Communism — all of which also base their pseudo-scientific justification on evolutionism.

While dealing in this chapter with the more personal impact of evolutionism on human beings, however, we should explore a little more deeply into the subjects of abortionism, the "sexual revolution" as generated by Freudian "psychobabble," and anti-social behavior in general.

The "Free Choice" of Abortion

The modern euphemism for abortion has become the noble-sounding phrase, "a woman's right to choose" — referring, of course, to her supposed right to abort her baby if she wants to do so. Most professing Christians, especially those who take the Bible literally as the authoritative Word of God, believe that abortion is actually murder of an unborn child, and so they must oppose it. The advocates of "freedom-of-choice," naturally, do not like to think of abortion as murder, and so insist that the "fetus" is not really human until it is born, or at least until about the third trimester of pregnancy. This, however, is quite wrong.

Unfortunately, a terrible holocaust of abortionism has been unleashed on our nation in recent years as a result of decisions by a humanist-dominated court system. What once was considered a serious crime is now considered a "human right" — that is, the so-called right of the mother to control her own body. Little, if any, consideration is

---

[14] Gould, *Ever Since Darwin,* p. 218, 223. Again, to prevent misunderstanding, Gould is merely citing — not approving — this idea.

given to the rights of the unborn child, for the simple reason that the fetus is now regarded as "not fully human." The basis of this inhuman decision is simply the evolutionary view of man, along with the "recapitulation theory," as briefly discussed above.

> So the abortion debate has its roots in two alternative ways of imagining the unborn. Our civilization, until recently, agreed in imagining the unborn child on the pattern of the incarnation, which maximizes his dignity; but many people now imagine him on the pattern of evolution, as popularly understood, which minimizes his dignity.[15]

This "pattern of evolution" as popularly understood is nothing else than the hoary evolutionary belief that "ontogeny recapitulates phylogeny." As Sobran says:

> The adage has been discredited, of course, but this does not mean it has lost its power over the imagination of many modern people. They still suppose that the human fetus is in the early stages of development a "lower" form of life, and this is probably what they mean when they say it isn't "fully human." It begins as something virtually amoebic, proceeds to become something like a shrimp, then a puppy, then an ape, and finally a human.[16]

If the embryo is merely recapitulating the animal stages of its evolutionary ancestry, then it is all right to terminate it before it becomes human, so the reasoning goes. The fact is, however, that this bizarre and self-serving notion has long since been disproved. As noted previously, leading evolutionist S. J. Gould admitted the following, while commenting on the recapitulation theory:

> In Down's day, the theory of recapitulation embodied a biologist's best guide for the organization of life into sequences of higher and lower forms. (Both the theory and "ladder approach" to classification that it encouraged are, or should be, defunct today).[17]

This most bizarre of the supposed evidences for organic evolution was popularized in the 19th century by the atheistic biologist Ernst Haeckel, who also headed Germany's infamous Monist League. The

[15] Joseph Sobran, "The Averted Gaze," p. 6. Sobran is a nationally syndicated columnist.
[16] *Ibid.*
[17] Gould, "Dr. Down's Syndrome," p. 144.

human embryo was said to begin life as a protozoan, then go through a fish stage (with gill slits) and a monkey stage (with a tail) before finally becoming a human being.

This absurd theory has long since been repudiated by competent biologists, even though it still appears in some textbooks and anti-creationist polemics. Any diminishing hope that it might be true should have been demolished by modern fetoscopy, which "makes it possible to observe directly the unborn child through a tiny telescope inserted through the uterine wall." Dr. Sabine Schwabenthan concludes:

> We now know, for instance, that man, in his prenatal stages, does not go through the complete evolution of life — from a primitive single cell to a fish-like water creature to man. Today it is known that every step in the fetal development process is specifically human.[18]

For a false notion, however, the recapitulation theory has had profound and tragic consequences. During the early days of paleontology, "progressive creationist" geologists such as Agassiz and D'Orbigny, following Cuvier, frequently used it as a framework for arranging their fossils in what they assumed should be a chronological sequence, on their simple assumption that God's successive creations should conform to their arrangement for classifying animals, and also to the embryological development of each animal.

The paleontological series so constructed naturally later seemed to give a superficial appearance of evolution, even though it included no real "transitional" forms, and even though it had little relation to any vertical successions of sedimentary strata. It was by this questionable device that the "fossil record," so constructed, later began to be cited as the main proof of evolution.

Also, as Harvard's Stephen Jay Gould has pointed out:

> Recapitulation provided a convenient focus for the pervasive racism of white scientists; they looked to the activities of their own children for comparison with normal, adult behavior in lower races.[19]

According to Gould, the term "mongoloid" was first applied to mentally defective people because it was then commonly believed that the Mongoloid race had not yet evolved to the status of the Caucasian

---

[18] Sabine Schwabenthan, "Life Before Birth," *Parents* (October 1979), p. 50.
[19] Gould, "Dr. Down's Syndrome," p. 144.

race. Similarly, Henry Fairfield Osborn, one of the leading American paleontologists of the first half of the 20th century, argued thus:

> The Negroid stock is even more ancient than the Caucasian and Mongolian. . . . The standard of intelligence of the average adult Negro is similar to that of the eleven-year-old youth of the species *Homo sapiens*.[20]

Osborn was director of the American Museum of Natural History at the time. As noted above, Haeckel (and his disciple Adolph Hitler) used the same false assumption of recapitulationsim to justify the myth of the Aryan super race, destined to subjugate or obliterate other races!

But all these tragic results of this false theory are dwarfed by the painful murders of millions of unborn children. Since 1973 over 35 million babies have been murdered by abortion, more than five times the number of Jews slain by the Nazis under Hitler. The only possible "scientific" rationalization for these atrocities is the standard argument that the unborn fetus is not yet really a human being at all, a widespread belief that can be based only on the evolutionary philosophy in general and this same old discredited recapitulation theory in particular. After all, it is not considered murder to kill mere animals.

Ideas do have consequences, and false ideas can have tragic and lethal consequences. The slogan "ontogeny recapitulates phylogeny" is not only a curious and discredited slogan of the past. It is also the root of a tree bearing deadly fruit in the present.

> Though it may still surprise some, there are few things more certain . . . than that the unborn are human beings. It is a biological and scientific fact that human life begins at fertilization, when the sperm cell of the father penetrates the egg cell of the mother. That unique genetic passage, something that each of us once was, contains everything that a person will become — the color of his eyes, the size of his feet, even whether or not he or she will contract diabetes at age fifty.
>
> Thanks to the wonders of modern technology, we are able to study the unborn child from the earliest moments of its existence. We know that its heart begins to beat eighteen days after fertilization, that brain waves can be recorded by the fortieth day, and that all body systems are present at

[20] Henry Fairfield Osborn, "The Evolution of Human Races," *Natural History* (January/February 1926), reprinted in *Natural History* (April 1980), p. 129.

eight weeks and are working by the eleventh week.[21]

The Bible also teaches that each human conceptus is a true human being, with an eternal soul, right from the moment of conception. The only pseudo-scientific rationale for teaching otherwise is the long-discredited recapitulation theory. The embryo does *not* go through the assumed evolutionary stages of its ancestors, for there were never any such evolutionary stages anyhow. It is never an amoeba, never a fish with gill slits, never a monkey with a tail, never anything but a human being! Abortionism is nothing but an evil fruit of the evolutionary tree.

Evolutionary Psychology and the Sexual Revolution

Although sexual immorality has been a problem in every age and every culture, it has always, at least in Christian societies, been recognized as wrong. In America, for example, there have been laws against adultery, abortion, pornography, and homosexuality, as well as incest, bestiality, and other sexual crimes. Pre-marital chastity and marital fidelity have been the standard (though not always maintained) in the past, but nowadays these virtues are considered by many people to be passé — in fact, almost an occasion for ridicule.

No doubt, many contributing factors have brought about this wholesale change in our sexual mores, but a major factor undoubtedly has been the explosive growth of the psychological and counseling professions. Practitioners in these fields have — ever since Freud in particular — by and large promoted the idea that most human psychological problems are caused by society's sexual inhibitions. Therefore, such inhibitions are considered harmful and should be removed. Since sexual freedom — even promiscuity — is normal behavior among most animals, and since we are merely higher animals, this should be our norm also, many would argue.

Although many of the teachings of Sigmund Freud have been challenged by present-day psychologists and psychiatrists, this animalistic idea is still their basic premise, and is taught in almost all the educational programs preparing men and women for these professions. The explosive proliferation of "counselors" in the current generation — even in seminaries and churches — has been a remarkable sign of the times. And, once again, evolutionism is the root of it all.

Sigmund Freud is often listed together with Charles Darwin and Karl Marx as the three men whose teachings have had the greatest impact on the modern world. Furthermore, both Marx and Freud acknowledged

[21] James J. Drimmey, "Abortion: the Other Holocaust," *The New American*, vol. 2, January 20, 1986), p. 22.

their indebtedness to Darwin. The role of Marx is discussed in the next chapter, but Freud is even more an intellectual child of Darwin than Marx. Freud, in turn, is a sort of grandfather of the modern sexual revolution, basing many of his libidinous teachings on the recapitulation theory as advocated by Darwin and then popularized, on the continent especially, by Ernst Haeckel — Darwin's European "bulldog" — in Germany.

> Evidently influenced by Haeckel, Freud believed that each person's history from fetus to adult recapitulates in brief the entire development of the human race. Both libido and ego, Freud argued, "are at bottom heritages, abbreviated recapitulations of the development which all mankind has passed through from its primeval days." . . . Freud thought that individual libidinal development recapitulates stages of human civilization. He believed that he could reconstruct human prehistory from studying children, as well as from observing neurotics.[22]

Like Darwin and Marx, Freud was almost obsessed with hostility toward Christianity and the Bible, especially their moral teachings. A modern conservative scholar, Dr. Paul Vitz, has recently published an important analysis of this aspect of Freud's life and thought in his book *Sigmund Freud's Christian Unconscious*. A reviewer of the Vitz book comments as follows:

> [Vitz] develops the claim that Freud had a strong attraction to Christianity. A corollary emphasis treats of Freud's unconscious hostility toward the Faith, which, as Vitz details, was a consequence of a curious preoccupation with the Devil, Damnation and the Anti-Christ.[23]

It is curious that both Darwin and Marx had made a profession of faith in Christ as young men, but later turned bitterly against this youthful profession. What was once an "attraction to Christianity" turned to hatred when they resisted the moral implications, and they then tried to justify this reaction by appealing to "science." In Freud's case,

---

[22] Martin Schatzman, "Freud's Debt to Darwin," review of *Darwin's Influence on Freud: A Tale of Two Sciences*, by Lucille B. Ritvo (New Haven, CT: Yale University Press, 1990), in *New Scientist*, vol. 129, (February 9, 1991), p. 62.

[23] G. A. Cevasco, "Freud versus God," review of *Sigmund Freud's Christian Unconscious*, by Paul C. Vitz (New York, NY: Guilford Press, 1988), in *Intercollegiate Review*, vol. 24 (Fall 1988), p. 39.

as in that of Marx, this reaction became exceedingly bitter.

> At every point, Vitz turns introspective eyes back onto Freud in order to expose the psychological motives for his rejection of God. Vitz even questions if Freud made a Faustian pact with the devil.[24]

What was true of Freud became true of multitudes of his followers in succeeding generations, at least in their total rejection of the Christian faith and biblical moral standards. They assumed, erroneously, that Freud had disproved the validity of Christianity, especially in view of the "science" of evolution.

> That Freud disproved religion, Vitz makes clear, is an overstated and oversimplified judgment bandied about by superficially educated and tragically uninformed individuals.[25]

Nevertheless, his successors in the fields of psychology and psychiatry have, with few exceptions, followed him in building their own systems on evolutionism and the repudiation of biblical morality. A typical example is the clinical professor of psychiatry at McMaster University, who has proclaimed:

> Christian doctrine, the existential soother par excellence, is incompatible with the principles of sound mental health.[26]

It is not only the psychologists, but also practically all the social scientists (cultural anthropologists, sociologists, etc.) who hold such views today. The editor of the *Anthropology and Humanism Quarterly* is a strong critic of what he considers fundamentalist morality.

> The doctrine of creationism and the attendant values involving rigid adherence to moral purity are impervious to arguments of reason.[27]

He does at least recognize that creationism and moral purity are directly related. Evolutionism, with its premise that men and women are

---

[24] *Ibid.*, p. 40.

[25] *Ibid.*

[26] Wendell W. Walters, "Christianity and Mental Health," *The Humanist*, vol. 47 (November/December 1987), p. 5.

[27] Bruce T. Grindal, "Creationism, Sexual Purity, and the Religious Right," *The Humanist*, vol. 43 (March/April 1983), p. 19.

merely evolved animals, provides the perfect pseudo-scientific rationale for those who would do away with such scripturally based restraints.

All of these evil conclusions are implicit in the basic tenets of evolutionary humanism, which is the (unofficial but nevertheless quite real) established religion of our public educational institutions and of most of the major private schools and colleges of our country. It is also the basic premise of almost all practicing psychologists — except for those few who specifically found their counsel on biblical teachings and principles.

When the 15 so-called "Tenets of Humanism" were first developed in 1933, largely through the influence of the famous philosopher/psychologist/educator John Dewey, and published as the "Humanist Manifesto," it was significant that the first 2 "Tenets" constituted a statement of faith in the evolutionary origin of the universe and of man, respectively.

The second "Humanist Manifesto," published in 1973, was built on the first and updated to the standards of the "enlightened" sixties and seventies. It dealt at some length with 17 spheres of concern to society, number six of which was "the area of sexuality." This section began with the following affirmation:

> We believe that intolerant attitudes, often cultivated by orthodox religions and puritanical cultures, unduly repress sexual conduct.

It went on to declare:

> Short of harming others or compelling them to do likewise, individuals should be permitted to express their sexual proclivities and pursue their lifestyles as they desire.[28]

In other words, anything goes in sex, short of rape or enforced prostitution. There is nothing wrong with fornication, promiscuity, adultery, homosexuality, incest, or even pederasty or bestiality, as long as all participants agree and no one is hurt. After all, animals do these things, and humans are merely evolved animals, so why not? The Bible and Christianity say that they are wrong and will be subject to divine punishment, but "science" has cleverly freed us from such "orthodox religions and puritanical cultures" in this modern age. So they say, but

[28] Both Humanist Manifest I and Humanist Manifesto II have been published in many places. They may be obtained, for example, from The Humanist Bookstore, 1780 S. Bellaire St., Denver, CO 80222.

the explosive growth of sexually transmitted diseases — especially AIDS — as well as divorce, child abuse, and a host of other ills, suggests that an initial wave of divine judgment may already be taking place.

One of the most distressing developments on the modern scene is the breakdown of the institution of the family. In some states there are now at least as many divorces as there are marriages. A large proportion of troubled juveniles are known to come from broken homes. Even many families that manage to stay together seem to experience almost continual bickering and angry clashing, with no clear-cut lines of authority and with low standards of moral behavior.

It is no mere coincidence that this modern deterioration of family life has occurred contemporaneously with the modern universal prevalence of evolutionary teaching. After all, God's creation and man's family life are closely associated in the Bible! The institution of marriage was the first human institution established by God, and the command to have children was God's first commandment to man (Gen. 1:27-28).

Because of the close relation of the home and family to God's creation, it is not surprising when we note today that a sound concept of marital and parental responsibilities goes hand-in-glove with a sound concept of biblical creationism.

Similarly, it is no mere coincidence that the ascendancy of evolutionary philosophy in the past century was quickly followed by the decline of the sanctity of the home and marriage relationships. If man is not the special creation of God, then neither is the home. If man is an evolved animal, then the morals of the barnyard and the jungle are more "natural," and therefore more "healthy" than the artificially imposed restrictions of premarital chastity and marital fidelity. Instead of monogamy, why not promiscuity and polygamy? Instead of training children in the nurture and admonition of the Lord, better to teach them how to struggle and survive in a cut-throat world, and then toss them out of the nest. Self-preservation is the first law of nature; only the fittest will survive. Be the cock-of-the-walk and the king-of-the-mountain! Eat, drink, and be merry, for life is short and that's the end. So says evolution!

Perhaps the greatest indictment of all against evolution is this assault against permanent, monogamous marriage and the sacred obligation of parents and children to each other. A strong emphasis on the full doctrine of biblical creationism, in all its implications (including the proper biblical roles of husband and wife) in both the home and church, is the best investment that can be made toward a happy home life, both in one's own home and in the future homes of one's children, and ultimately toward a healthy society and preparation for eternal responsibilities.

Undoubtedly, many personal and cultural reasons exist for the deterioration of family life in modern society, and most of them can be shown to stem from the naturalistic, evolutionary philosophy that has been indoctrinated in young people for two generations or more through the schools and the media of mass communication. Perhaps the most important such factor involved in this breakdown has been the so-called "sexual revolution."

Pornography in almost every form is now freely available to all comers, not only in R-rated movies and newsstand paperbacks, but even on national television and in public school textbooks. People are constantly intimidated by "scientific" surveys which purportedly show majorities of both single and married people participating in pre-marital and extra-marital sex adventures, with the persuasive implication that what is done by "everyone" must be normal and therefore right for everyone.

The fact that sex outside of a permanent marriage bond is contrary to Scripture and to God's revealed will (note Heb. 13:4; Eph. 5:3-5; Matt. 19:3-9; etc.) is considered by evolutionists to be irrelevant, since the Bible is believed to be merely a product of man's religious evolution in an earlier stage of history and therefore no longer authoritative in our modern age of enlightenment and freedom.

Furthermore, since most animals are indiscriminate with regard to partners in mating and, since men and women are believed to have evolved from animals, then why shouldn't we *live* like animals? Why develop sexual inhibitions and frustrations that may lead to psychological neuroses?

The modern psychological systems of Freud, Watson, Skinner, Rogers, and other leaders of the different schools of psychological thought today are all (whether Freudian, behavioristic, humanistic, or whatever may be the current fad in this field) based on the assumption that man is an animal, the product of ages of evolutionary struggle.

On this assumption, people are counseled to release the sexual inhibitions that have been imposed on them by religion and act "naturally" (which, interpreted, means to follow all their animal instincts) and engage in whatever sexual activity they desire, with as many partners (of either sex) as they wish. Any unwanted children resulting from such activity can, of course, be taken care of either by abortion or by becoming wards of the state. Some are now even proposing infanticide, the disposal of children after birth.

The concern expressed by Christian parents and pastors over the widespread introduction of sex education courses into the public schools is precisely because of the prominence of this kind of emphasis (sex as natural, with no moral connotations, based on the assumption of human evolution from an animal ancestry) in the texts and courses offered.

The sad testimony of multitudes of broken homes and broken lives, in contrast with the joyful testimony of multitudes of truly Christian families, is proof enough that evolutionary theory and the sexual revolution philosophy that has been based on it are false and deadly. "A good tree cannot bring forth evil fruit, neither can a corrupt tree bring forth good fruit. Every tree that bringeth not forth good fruit is hewn down, and cast into the fire" (Matt. 7:18-19).

Homosexuality and the Drug Culture

Two other evil fruits of evolutionism are the modern promotion of homosexuality and the explosive increase of drug use, even in "Christian" America. These movements are combined in this section because they are both tied in closely to the sexual revolution, as it has been called, and also because they are the two main culprits in the great AIDS disease that many fear will eventually engulf the world.

While both homosexuality and drug abuse have been present throughout history, they have largely been confined to pagan cultures, where pantheistic evolutionism was the underlying philosophy justifying them. In Europe and America, on the other hand, where accepted social standards were largely built upon biblical morality, these practices were more or less hidden, confined to the anti-Christian occultic subculture that had never been fully eliminated by the professedly Christian majority world view based on creation.

With the sudden ascendance of Darwinian evolutionism in the West, however, these underground vices have become more and more prominent and acceptable even in Christendom, especially now that the materialistic evolutionism of the Darwinians is giving ground to the venerable pantheistic evolutionism of New Age philosophies and psychologies.

One of the most influential promoters of homosexual "rights" has been Dr. John Money, director of psychohormonal research at Johns Hopkins University, the location of one of the nation's most prestigious medical research installations. In a publication of the famous (or infamous) Kinsey Institute, Dr. Money acknowledges the reliance of the homosexual movement on evolutionism for its apparent justification:

> Any theory of the genesis of either exclusive homosexuality or exclusive heterosexuality must address primarily the genesis of bisexuality. Monosexuality, whether

> homosexual or heterosexual, is secondary and a derivative of the primary bisexual or ambisexual potential. Ambisexuality has its origins in evolutionary biology and in the embryology of sexual differentiation.[29]

It is assumed by Money that, since animals are bisexual and generally promiscuous, so too it is natural for their human evolutionary descendants to be bisexual and promiscuous. Money also says:

> Therefore, it is likely that acculturation to bisexuality is less a concomitant of inbreeding than it is of the bisexual plasticity of all members of the human species. It is possible that bisexual plasticity may vary over the life span. Later in life it may give way to exclusive monosexuality — or it may not.[30]

An article in a leading homosexual magazine also stresses the evolutionary "naturalness" of homosexual (or bisexual) behavior, as follows:

> Homosexuality is seldom discussed as a component in evolution, but it undoubtedly plays a role. Homosexual behavior has been observed in most animal species studied, and the higher we climb on the taxonomic tree toward mammals, the more apparent homosexual behavior we see.[31]

This author cites observations of such behavior in a wide variety of animal species — specifically mice, hummingbirds, seagulls, and chimpanzees. He suggests its supposed evolutionary advantages in humans as including both relief of tension and also population control!

Even such a "straight" evolutionist as Michael Ruse is ready to acknowledge that homosexuality is a "natural" behavior in animals and, therefore — by evolutionary criteria — in humans.

> Is homosexuality biologically unnatural? Modern evolutionary theory suggests that this claim is highly ques-

---

[29] John Money, "Agenda and Crescenda of the Kinsey Scale," chapter 4 in *Homosexuality/Heterosexuality: Concepts of Sexual Orientation,* ed. David P. McWhirter, Stephanie A. Sanders, and June M. Reinisch (New York, NY: Oxford University Press, 1990), p. 45.

[30] *Ibid.*, p. 43.

[31] Jacob Smit, "In the Beginning: Homosexuality and Evolution," *International Northwest Guide Magazine,* Issue 19 (August 1987), p. 6.

> tionable. Certainly we can say with some confidence that homosexual activity is not (as everyone from Plato on down seems to have assumed) a phenomenon exclusively restricted to humans. Indeed, it is no exaggeration to say that *every* animal species studied with care shows some such behavior.[32]

As a matter of fact, the Bible itself implies that homosexual behavior is something animals might do, when it applies the epithet of "dog" to the human homosexual (Deut. 23:17–18).

The difference, however, is that the Bible calls it "sin," rather than a natural evolutionary heritage. Whatever may or may not explain what evolutionists interpret as homosexual behavior in animals, such behavior is condemned by God in no uncertain terms in human beings. In the theocracy of ancient Israel, homosexuality was a capital crime (Lev. 20:13). It is also the object of severe condemnation in the New Testament (e.g., Rom. 1:24-28).

Despite the amazing propaganda machine currently promoting the notion that AIDS is as much a problem for heterosexuals as for homosexuals and drug users, the fact remains that, even after two decades of such propaganda, AIDS still affects almost exclusively those two groups — plus a few others infected by blood transfusions received from someone in one of these categories. One could certainly make the argument that AIDS is a divine judgment on those who deny God and His Word by this flagrant violation of His primeval standard for the human race as given to the first man and woman (see Gen. 2:22-24). That standard is permanent heterosexual monogamous marriage, preceded by premarital chastity and accompanied by marital fidelity. Evolutionism rejects both the primeval creation and this accompanying divine institution established by the Creator, and God will not be mocked forever.

As far as the explosive modern drug problem is concerned, this is largely a concomitant of the modern sexual revolution, with each tending to promote and accompany the other. To the degree that drug use has any kind of scientific rationale, however, once again we find evolutionary thinking at the root of it.

The evolutionary connection is not as obvious as with some of the other corrupt fruits, of course, because no one suggests that drugs contributed to evolution of the species (de-volution, perhaps!).

---

32 Michael Ruse, "Evolutionary Theory and Christian Ethics: Are They in Harmony?" *Zygon*, vol. 29 (March 1994), p. 10.

There is an important indirect connection, however. Evolutionism has made God redundant, intellectually at least. Yet, emotionally, people still have a deep-seated need for some sense of meaning to life beyond the hum-drum of everyday living. In the ancient religions (which, as we have noted, were based on evolutionary pantheism), intellectuals found this in a sort of mystical communion with the cosmic "deity," with Mother Nature, as it were. The common people did essentially the same, only with different specific emanations of that deity, in the form of particular idols representing particular attributes of the deified cosmos. Very often, this experience was stimulated or intensified with drugs (or "sorceries," as the Greek word *pharmakeis*, from which we get "pharmacy," is translated in the New Testament).

Christians, of course, can enjoy genuine communion with God through the indwelling Holy Spirit of God, received by faith in Christ and His redeeming work. Others, however, must seek something else to fill the "God-shaped vacuum" in their souls. Since, in the thinking of brain-washed young people indoctrinated in evolution, God does not even exist, they tend to seek a spiritual experience or feeling some other way. Drugs give them a "high," an experience above themselves, and this is their substitute for fellowship with their Creator.

That, at least, was the teaching of the forerunners and intellectual promoters of the use of hallucinatory drugs — men such as Aldous Huxley and Timothy Leary — and millions have followed these false prophets.

Aldous Huxley, like his brother Julian, was an avowed evolutionist and atheist. He wrote many books along such lines, but his attitude and teachings on this matter were well summarized in an article in *Scientific Monthly*.

> But the pharmacologists will give us something that most human beings have never had before. If we want joy, peace, and lovingkindness, they can give us lovingkindness, peace, and joy. If we want beauty, they will transfigure the outside world for us and open the door to visions of unimaginable richness and significance. If our desire is for life everlasting, they will give us the next best thing — eons of blissful experience miraculously telescoped into a single hour. They will bestow these gifts without exacting the terrible price which, in the past, man had to pay for resorting too frequently to such consciousness-changing

> drugs as heroin or cocaine or even that good old standby alcohol.[33]

It does seem to such intellectuals that heaven itself can be provided — without the cross of Christ — by these new drugs the pharmacologists will develop!

Huxley wrote those words almost 40 years ago, and his followers are still waiting. The drugs can give them strange experiences all right, but there is still a "terrible price" to pay! Huxley still had faith that these future wonder drugs would provide a satisfying substitute for God and His salvation.

> Meanwhile, all that one can predict with any degree of certainty is that many of our traditional notions about ethics and religion and many of our current views about the nature of the mind will have to be reconsidered and re-evaluated in the context of the pharmacological revolution.[34]

Tooth and Claw

In the next chapter, we shall consider the effect of evolutionary teaching on the broad conflicts between nations, between races, and between social orders. These have been profound and have been the cause of great suffering throughout history.

Furthermore, these widespread conflicts have naturally had their counterparts in local battles. As the Apostle James reminds us: "From whence come wars and fightings among you? come they not hence, even of your lusts that war in your members? Ye lust, and have not: ye kill, and desire to have, and cannot obtain" (James 4:1-2). The root problem, of course, is sin, and both people and nations have been fighting one another all through history, but never since the days of Noah on the fearsome scale that exists today.

There have always been local wars, but now there are global wars, in addition to scores of local conflicts. There have always been robbers and murderers, but now there is organized crime on a vast scale that even controls governments. There have always been individual rebels and law breakers, but now the schools must be patrolled by policemen, and the streets are unsafe everywhere, even in "Christian" nations such as America.

But what could one expect after a century of teaching in our

---

[33] Aldous Huxley, "History of Tension," *Scientific Monthly* (July 1957), p. 9.
[34] *Ibid.*

schools that denies God and the Bible, outlaws the Ten Commandments, encourages sexual promiscuity, and promotes self-centeredness, all in the revered name of "science," the euphemism for evolutionism? If individuals and groups are taught continually that progress has come about by way of a "nature red in tooth and claw" (Tennyson), that there is always a "struggle for existence" and the results of that struggle have led to "survival of the fittest," how can such teaching *not* affect both individual behavior and national policy?

This is easily documented in the case of wars and racism and class struggle, as shown in the next chapter. It may not be so easy to document in individual instances, of course, because people commit sin for all kinds of personal reasons, but the background cause is surely lack of fear of God, as well as either ignorance or rejection of God's standards. "And even as they did not like to retain God in their knowledge, God gave them over to a reprobate mind, to do those things which are not convenient" (Rom. 1:28). "There is no fear of God before their eyes" (Rom. 3:18).

Once again, all this goes back to the underlying assumption that any personal responsibility to a Creator has been outmoded by modern evolutionism. As a matter of fact, this situation has existed in all those societies, both ancient and modern, built around pantheistic evolutionism, as well as those modern "Christian" societies that have largely capitulated to atheistic Darwinian evolutionism. It is hard to think of a more reasonable explanation than just this for the moral and social chaos that is now plaguing American society. In a book appropriately titled *Created from Animals*, philosopher James Rachels puts it this way:

> Darwinism undermines both the idea that man is made in the image of God and the idea that man is a uniquely rational being. Furthermore, if Darwinism is correct, it is unlikely that any other support for the idea of human dignity will be found. The idea of human dignity turns out, therefore, to be the moral effluvium of a discredited metaphysics.[35]

This type of evil in society, the use of violence to obtain what one desires, has frequently been justified by evolutionary reasoning. Ever since Raymond Dart discovered the first fossil of *Australopithecus* in the mid-1920s, along with what he thought were "tools" used by these so-called "hominids" (or supposed ape-like ancestors of man), it has been widely held that these creatures were carnivorous "killer apes," who

[35] James Rachels, *Created from Animals* (New York, NY: Oxford University Press, 1990), p. 5. Rachels is professor of philosophy at the University of Alabama.

slaughtered animals and probably other hominids for food and possibly for conquest or even sport.

This bloodthirsty attribute of these presumed humanoid ancestors of man supposedly "explains" and even "justifies" man's instinctive drive to conquer and loot and kill! This "caveman" caricature of ancient men and women has been inordinately popularized in comic strips and motion pictures and even school books for many years, but anthropologists now know that it is false. The bones of animals supposedly slaughtered, skinned, scraped, and eaten by the australopithecines had been misinterpreted all along.

> They concluded that the australopithecines, like the baboons and antelopes from the same deposits, had been dragged into the caves and eaten by leopards and carnivores. Most and probably all of the bone tools were scraps from a cat's lunch — and so were the remains of the supposed killer apes.[36]

Men and women may be prone to all sorts of violent and selfish behavior, but this is because of sin in their hearts, not animals in their ancestry. It needs to be condemned and judged, unless first repented, forgiven, and forsaken — not coddled and justified on the basis of evolutionary presuppositions, as even the courts have been so quick to do in recent decades.

Still another animalistic practice is now beginning to be advocated, on the basis of evolutionism. Once abortionism has become acceptable, infanticide cannot be far behind, as well as other "checks" on population growth (euthanasia, etc.).

> Among some animal species, then, infant killing appears to be a natural practice. Could it be natural for humans too, a trait inherited from our primate ancestors? . . . Charles Darwin noted in *The Descent of Man* that infanticide has been "probably the most important of all checks" on population growth throughout most of human history.[37]

There have already been many attempts even at genocide in the name of evolutionary progress, such as the slaughter of the aborigines in Tasmania by white settlers, who argued that these "primitives" were not really human, the gas ovens of Nazi Germany in the name

---

[36] Matt Cartmill, "Four Legs Good, Two Legs Bad," *Natural History*, vol. 92 (November 1983), p. 76.

[37] Barbara Burke, "Infanticide," *Science 84* (May 1984), p. 29.

of Aryan racial supremacy, and others.

If evolution is the real law of life, then practices such as these may really contribute to the overall progress of evolution, as their practitioners allege. It is hard to offer an effective scientific argument against them, if evolution is true.

A leading humanist philosopher and historian, Will Durant, made the following comments shortly before he died:

> By offering evolution in place of God as a cause of history, Darwin removed the theological basis of the moral code of Christendom. And the moral code that has no fear of God is very shaky. That's the condition we are in.[38]

The founding fathers of our great nation were God-fearing men, and our laws were based essentially on the laws of God as recorded in the Holy Scriptures. But we have now arrived at a situation where our traditional freedom *of* religion is interpreted by our courts and schools and media as freedom *from* religion (or at least freedom from the *true* religion of the Bible). It is no wonder that we are heading fast into chaos. As Will Durant put it:

> Order is the mother of liberty, liberty is the mother of chaos, chaos is the mother of dictatorship.[39]

---

[38] Will Durant, "We are in the Last Stage of a Pagan Period," *Chicago Tribune Syndicate* (April 1980).

[39] *Ibid.*

Chapter 4

Evolutionism and Its Deadly Social Philosophies

Many writers, both Christian and non-Christian, have pointed out the evolutionistic base of such deadly social philosophies as communism and Nazism, as well as racism and laissez-faire capitalism. Modern evolutionists react angrily when attention is called to this fact, but it *is* a fact, as can be easily confirmed in the literature of the theoreticians and practitioners of each of these systems.

In this chapter, we want to examine, in more or less the chronological order of their respective heydays, the following systems, all of which were rationalized by their founders and promoters as based on the premise of evolution. First, we shall consider "social Darwinism," the laissez-faire capitalistic system which developed along with so-called "scientific Darwinism" and had (and still has, in some degree) great influence in Europe and America, with spillover effects in Asia, Africa, and Australia. Then we shall look at modern racism, followed by Fascism and Nazism, then communism, and finally the New Age philosophies.

Social Darwinism

In the last half of the 19th century, a widespread philosophy known as social Darwinism dominated the thinking of many of the industrial tycoons of the era.

> As the steel magnate Andrew Carnegie put it after reading Darwin and Spencer: "Not only had I got rid of theology and the supernatural, but I had found the truth of evolution. *All is well since all grows better* became my

motto, my true source of comfort."[1]

Similar philosophies were expressed by such men as John D. Rockefeller, the oil baron; James Hill, the railroad magnate; and numerous others, all impressed by the teachings of Herbert Spencer in England and William Grant Sumner in the United States, epitomized by the famous slogan "struggle for existence and survival of the fittest."

This right-wing type of Darwinism also led to racism and imperialism, and even to Fascism and Hitlerism, whereas a left-wing approach to evolutionary thought became basic in Marxist-Leninism and Communism. Both systems are anti-creationist, anti-biblical, and anti-Christian, and even when they fight with each other, they remain united in opposition to creationism and biblical fundamentalism.

The familiar Darwinian bywords "struggle for existence" and "survival of the fittest" were not actually coined by Darwin, but by two of his immediate predecessors, Thomas Malthus and Herbert Spencer, respectively. Each of these men had a profound influence on Darwin's thinking, and he appropriated these slogans to his own use in trying to explain and promote his ideas of "natural selection" in the animal kingdom.

They were also ideally suited mottoes for exploitation by the industrialists and militarists of the 19th century in their own agendas.

> Spencer coined the phrase *survival of the fittest*, and Darwin adopted the parlance in later editions of his *Origin of Species*. . . . According to Spencer and his American disciples — business entrepreneurs like John D. Rockefeller and Andrew Carnegie — social hierarchy reflects the unwavering, universal laws of nature. Nature unfolds in such a way that the strong survive and the weak perish. Thus, the economic and social structures that survive are "stronger" and better, and those structures that don't were obviously meant to founder. It is *better* that capitalism has survived the Cold War just as it was better that the mammals survived the Mesozoic Era when dinosaurs became extinct. "How do we know that capitalism is better than Communism and that the mammal is better than the dinosaur? Because they survived, of course."[2]

---

[1] Cited in Edward Kirkland's "Introduction," Dale Carnegie, *The Gospel of Wealth* (Cambridge, MA: Harvard University Press, 1962).

[2] Stephen T. Asma, "The New Social Darwinism: Deserving Your Destitution," *The Humanist* (September/October 1993), p. 11.

Modern evolutionists, such as the author of the above quotation, today deplore the excesses of social Darwinism. The fact is, however, that it became very popular among the laissez-faire capitalists of the 19th century because it did, indeed, seem to give scientific sanction to ruthless competition in both business and politics. A current leader among evolutionary geologists is Dr. Kenneth Hsu, a Chinese scientist now teaching in Switzerland. He has frequently inveighed against Darwinism as a science, precisely because it sanctioned exploitation of his own people.

> Darwinism was also used in a defense of competitive individualism and its economic corollary of laissez-faire capitalism in England and in America. Andrew Carnegie wrote that "the law of competition, be it benign or not, is here; we cannot evade it." Rockefeller went a step further when he claimed that "the growth of a large business is merely a survival of the fittest; it is merely the working out of a law of nature and a law of God."[3]

Another modern evolutionist who would like to divest himself of the Darwinian heritage, even while retaining his commitment to evolutionism, is a prominent philosopher now at the University of Alabama. He writes as follows:

> "The survival of the fittest" was quickly interpreted as an ethical precept that sanctioned cutthroat economic competition.[4]

The fact that this evolutionary competition involved exploitation of labor — even child labor — as well as monopolistic elimination of smaller competitors, and even strong-arm tactics against dissenters, was justified as good in the long run, in the name of evolutionary "science."

> Capitalist giants such as John D. Rockefeller and Andrew Carnegie regularly invoked what they took to be "Darwinian" principles to explain the ethics of the American system. Rockefeller, in a talk to his Sunday school class, proclaims that . . . "the American Beauty rose can be produced in the splendor and fragrance which bring cheer to its beholder only by sacrificing the early buds which grow up around it." . . . Carnegie, who became a close

---

[3] Kenneth J. Hsu, "Darwin's Three Mistakes," *Geology*, vol. 14 (June 1986), p. 534.
[4] Rachels, *Created from Animals*, p. 63.

> friend of Spencer's, was equally rhapsodic: in defending the concentration of wealth in the hands of a few big businessmen, he proclaimed that "While the law may sometimes be hard for the individual, it is best for the race, because it ensures the survival of the fittest in every department."[5]

Both Rockefeller and Carnegie originally considered themselves to be Christians — though of liberal persuasion. Carnegie gave up his professed belief completely when he became a Darwinian.

> Andrew Carnegie, who practically worshipped Spencer, replaced his disenchanted Christian theology with the laissez-faire motto "All is well since all grows better." These capitalist moguls eagerly embraced a metaphysics that provided the ultimate justification for their ruthless business tactics.[6]

We have referred mainly to Rockefeller and Carnegie as the two best-known social Darwinists, but this attitude prevailed among many — probably most — of the business and industrial leaders of the capitalist countries. It is still true today among many leading political and economic "conservatives."

This "survival of the fittest" philosophy was also applied on the national scale. The western nations, in Europe especially, assumed that they had been proved the "fittest," and so assumed that they should subjugate and dominate the less "advanced" nations and tribes of the world. This imperialistic compulsion led to their supposed "white man's burden," involving exploration and conquest of many African, Asian, and Australian regions. Other motivations stimulated this desire for territorial expansion long before Darwin, of course — greed, ambition, even missionary zeal — but Darwinism (as well as earlier evolutionary philosophies) gave it an *apparent* scientific rationale.

Even today after many of these once-subject nations have been "liberated" and given self-rule, the more "advanced" nations still have a patronizing attitude toward the "third world," still trying to dominate them economically, if not militarily.

> The idea that whole populations — whether abroad or at home — are "naturally unfit" is the ultimate license for social policies of domination. Indeed, domination is for us

[5] Rachels, *Created from Animals*, p. 64.

[6] Asma, "New Social Darwinism," p. 11.

> a virtue rather than a vice. If one pauses for a moment to reflect on whether or not the "natural law of competition" is sound, then one is immediately suspected of impiety. The church of capitalism watches its flock carefully.[7]

It is worth noting, at least briefly, that social Darwinism also played an important role in Japanese imperialism. The exportation of Darwinism to Asia eventually resulted in communism in China, but Japan was more influenced by social Darwinism, as evinced, for example, by her alliance with Hitler in World War II.

A fascinating paper by Dr. Hiroshi Unoura, a social scientist on the Faculty of Arts and Sciences at Kitasato University in Tokyo, has outlined the development of social Darwinism in Japan, giving the reasons for its rapid acceptance and application. He notes that social Darwinism was accepted more rapidly in Japan than was biological evolutionism, because of the easy-to-understand ideas of struggle and survival. Evolutionism was officially promoted in the university system, using western-educated professors, in order to accelerate westernization of the culture and also to replace Japanese feelings of racial inferiority with feelings of superiority.[8]

Evolutionism was also promoted out of opposition to Christianity, since it was assumed that it was anti-Christian, despite the fact that some of the most influential Japanese Christians were promoting theistic evolutionism. Japanese Buddhists in particular promoted the assimilation of evolutionary theory into their Buddhist system, arguing thereby that Buddhism was more "scientific" than Christianity. Today, evolutionism dominates all the schools and universities of Japan, and the Japanese intellectuals now tend to believe that, in the Darwinian struggle, they are no longer an inferior race, but superior to the Caucasians.

Ultimate Evolutionism — Nazism and the Master Race

Though not much in vogue currently, the fascistic systems of Hitler, Mussolini, and others almost conquered the world a generation ago. There are even now neo-Nazi movements that bear watching, as well as various dictatorships of similar character around the world — not to mention the "new left" student movement of the sixties and seventies, which strangely resembled the early days of Nazism.

In any case, all such ideologies, built up as they are on the concepts

---

[7] *Ibid.*, p. 12.

[8] Hiroshi Unoura, "Samurai Darwinism: A Reception and Development of Social Darwinism in Early Modern Japan." Unpublished paper presented at the Japan Forum, Harvard/M.I.T. (March 12, 1993).

of racism and statist totalitarian aggression and control, are direct products of the Darwinian doctrines of struggle for existence and survival of the fittest. Friedrich Nietzsche, the philosophical father of these systems, was an ardent evolutionist, as were his spiritual children, Hitler and Mussolini.

> From the "Preservation of Favoured Races in the Struggle for Life" (i.e., Darwin's subtitle to *Origin of Species*) it was a short step to the preservation of favored individuals, classes, or nations — and from their preservation to their glorification. Social Darwinism has often been understood in this sense: as a philosophy, exalting competition, power, and violence over convention, ethics, and religion. Thus it has become a portmanteau of nationalism, imperialism, militarism and dictatorship, of the cults of the hero, the superman, and the master race . . . recent expressions of this philosophy, such as (Hitler's) *Mein Kampf*, are, unhappily, too familiar to require exposition here. And it is by an obvious process of analogy and deduction that they are said to derive from Darwinism. . . . Nietzsche predicted that this would be the consequence if the Darwinian theory gained general acceptance.[9]

It might be appropriate to refer again (footnote 30, chapter 1), at this point, to the classic volume on evolutionary ethics by Sir Arthur Keith. When he wrote his book, he had just been through World War II, enduring with other Britons the awful suffering visited by Adolph Hitler on England and the world. He certainly did not write out of any feeling of sympathy for Hitler and his cause. Yet his correct understanding of the real nature of evolution, in which he firmly and fully believed, impelled him to say the following:

> To see evolutionary measures and tribal morality being applied vigorously to the affairs of a great modern nation, we must turn again to Germany of 1942. We see Hitler devoutly convinced that evolution produces the only real basis for a national policy. . . . The means he adopted to secure the destiny of his race and people were organized slaughter, which has drenched Europe in blood. . . . Such conduct is highly immoral as measured by every scale of

---

[9] Gertrude Himmelfarb, *Darwin and the Darwinian Revolution* (London: Chatto and Windus Publ., 1959), p. 343-44.

> ethics, yet Germany justifies it; it is consonant with tribal or evolutionary morality. Germany has reverted to the tribal past, and is demonstrating to the world, in their naked ferocity, the methods of evolution.[10]

Continuing, Keith lauds political evolutionism thus:

> The German Fuhrer, as I have consistently maintained, is an evolutionist; he has consciously sought to make the practice of Germany conform to the theory of evolution. He has failed, not because the theory of evolution is false, but because he had made three fatal blunders in its application.[11]

Modern American evolutionists may be embarrassed by this philosophical association with the Fascism and Nazism of Mussolini and Hitler, but it is nevertheless a fact, and it is a fact that certainly ought to awaken *theistic* evolutionists, at least, to the real nature of the theory with which they have been willing to become identified for the sake of academic prestige. If one really feels he must believe in evolution, he should at least leave God out of it. The very idea of "theistic" evolution is a contradiction in terms, an oxymoron, like "theistic atheism" or "flaming snowflakes." The evil fruits of evolution are strong evidence of its bitter roots.

The Christian philosopher Francis Schaeffer has commented incisively on the Darwinian basis of German militarism and Nazism:

> Later, these ideas helped produce an even more far-reaching yet logical conclusion: the Nazi movement in Germany. Heinrich Himmler (1900-1945), leader of the Gestapo, stated that the law of nature must take its course in the survival of the fittest. The result was the gas chambers. Hitler stated numerous times that Christianity and its notion of charity should be "replaced by the ethic of strength over weakness." . . . Thus, many factors created the situation. But in that setting the theory of the survival of the fittest sanctioned what occurred.[12]

One of the most remarkable aspects of the rise of Hitler and the Nazis is that it was strongly encouraged and promoted by the German

---

[10] Sir Arthur Keith, *Evolution and Ethics* (New York, NY: Putnam, 1947), p. 28.
[11] *Ibid.*, p. 230.
[12] Francis Schaeffer, *How Should We Then Live?* (New York, NY: Revel, 1976), p. 151.

scientific establishment. Evolutionary scientists in America may decry the excesses of German militarism under the Kaiser in World War I and Hitler in World War II, but these were fully accepted and implemented by the German scientists of those periods. These men, often considered even in the West as outstanding scientists, were all Darwinian and Haeckelian evolutionists, building on the immoral foundation laid down especially by Nietzsche and Haeckel, back in Darwin's day.

It is well-known that the event that convinced the great liberal statesman William Jennings Bryan that he should devote the energies of his later years to fighting evolutionism was when he learned that the German militarists who had led their country into provoking and fighting the First World War had been inspired to do so by their belief in Darwinism as the key to national struggle and supremacy.

Hitler, after World War I, was even more firmly committed to evolutionism than any German leader before him. He was the ultimate evolutionist, if ever there was such a person. But he also was firmly backed by the evolutionary scientists of Germany, who had become convinced followers of Ernst Haeckel and Charles Darwin. It was their conviction that the Germans were destined to be one of the most "favored races in the struggle for life," as Darwin had expressed it, and so they proceeded to develop their scientific studies and political policies accordingly.

A revealing book, appropriately entitled *Murderous Science*, was written by Benno Muller-Hull and published by Oxford University Press in 1988. Reviewing this book, the American anthropologist Robert Proctor comments as follows:

> The thesis of the work is that "human genetics played a crucial role in the atrocities committed by the Nazis."
>
> Evidence for this claim is powerful, and disturbing, Eugene Fischer, for example, as head of the Kaiser Wilhelm Institute for Anthropology, Human Genetics and Eugenics (1927-1942), supervised the training of SS physicians and helped to administer the sterilization of German-Negro half-breeds in the Rhineland.[13]

Proctor himself has written incisively on this same theme. Matt Cartmill, of the Duke University Department of Biological Anthropology, in a review of a symposium on anthropology also published

---

[13] Robert N. Proctor, "Science and Nazism." Review of *Murderous Science*, by Benno Muller-Hull (New York, NY: Oxford University Press, 1988), *Science*, vol. 241 (Aug. 5, 1988), p. 730.

in 1988, has comments on Proctor's studies:

> In his lucid and disturbing chapter, "From *Anthropologie* to *Rassenkunde*," Robert Proctor traces the development of physical anthropology in Germany from a medical anatomists' hobby into the clinical specialty of *Rassenhygiene*. He shows how the major German societies of physical anthropologists collaborated with the SS program of race hygiene, helping to make racial policy, train SS physicians, and organize Gestapo sterilization programs. Eugene Fischer, the most distinguished of German physical anthropologists, regarded by many as the founder of human genetics, was particularly helpful in these efforts.[14]

Proctor, reviewing Muller-Hull's book, makes the following cogent observation:

> Muller-Hull stresses that Nazi racial policy was the work of trained scholars, not ignorant fanatics: how else are we to interpret the fact that 7 out of 14 participants at the notorious Wannsee conference (outlining plans for the "final solution") possessed doctorates, or that leading German psychiatrists were mobilized with hardly a single protest to exterminate Germany's mentally ill?[15]

George Stein concurs that German racial policies were based on what the German scientists taught as sound science.

> National socialism . . . was ultimately the first fully self-conscious attempt to organize a political community on a basis of an explicit biopolicy: a biopolicy fully congruent (or so it was claimed) with the scientific facts of the Darwinian revolution.[16]

Robert Proctor, continuing with his review of the remarkable book *Murderous Science*, comments as follows:

> Much of this book reads as a catalog of horrors. We

[14] Matt Cartmill, "Misdeeds in Anthropology." Review of *Bones, Bodies, Behavior: Essays on Biological Anthropology*, ed. George W. Stocking, Jr. (Wisconsin University Press, 1988), *Science*, vol. 244 (May 19, 1989), p. 858.

[15] Robert N. Proctor, "Science and Nazism," p. 731.

[16] George J. Stein, "Biological Science and the Roots of Nazism," *American Scientist*, vol. 76 (January/February 1988), p. 52.

> read how scholars at the Kaiser Wilhelm Institute for Brain Research scrambled to obtain the brains of murdered mentally ill (for purposes of dissection), and how the German Association for Scientific Research (DFG) provided support for Otmar von Verscheur, Fischer's successor at the Kaiser Wilhelm Institute for Anthropology, to have his assistant, Josef Mengele, prepare and ship eyes, blood, and other body parts back to Berlin for analysis.[17]

That such "horrors" are not unthinkable even in America is evident from the current push by U.S. scientists to make aborted fetuses available for scientific research, or even to produce embryos in the laboratory merely for research.

And, speaking of Josef Mengele, this immoral monster was in charge of the racial purification program at Auschwitz, yet was a highly respected scientist. He held both a Ph.D. from the prestigious University of Munich and an M.D. from the University of Frankfort. Two of his biographers note that his zeal was based on "mainline science theory," not on alleged sadistic and psychopathic tendencies in his nature.

> His real interest in genetics and evolution happened to coincide with the developing concept that some human beings afflicted by disorders were unfit to reproduce, even to live. . . . His consummate ambition was to succeed in this fashionable new field of evolutionary research.[18]

Eventually, in the eyes of Nazi evolutionary scientists, those "unfit to live" came to include not only people who were mentally ill or physically handicapped, but also Jews, Negroes, gypsies, and any others who did not have "pure" Teutonic genealogies. All of this was considered to be in the ultimate interest of the evolutionary advance of — as Darwin had put it — "the preservation of favored races in the struggle for life."

Hitler continually emphasized this concept of evolutionistic struggle in his own writings. In fact, the very title of his definitive book, *Mein Kampf*, meant "My Struggle." Hitler and his Nazis were the true evolutionists, in the fullest sense. As Stein says:

> The Germans, who focused on selection and the "struggle," or *Kampf* as it was translated, were closer to the

[17] Robert N. Proctor, "Science and Nazism," p. 731.

[18] G.L. Posner and J. Ware, *Mengele* (New York, NY: McGraw-Hill Book Co., 1986), p. 23.

radical insight of Darwin's efforts.[19]

Thus, German scientists — especially the geneticists, anthropologists, and psychiatrists, all firm believers in Darwinism — played a vital role in the atrocities of Hitler's Germany. And the frightening concomitant is that, at least until Hitler's actual military aggressions got under way, American and British scientists (who were also, for the most part, evolutionary racists at that time) seemed to approve this philosophy, or at least to condone it, in the name of science.

> But surely American physical anthropologists spoke out clearly against the Nazi perversion of their science? They did not. Elazar Barkan's chapter relates their failure in depressing detail.[20]

Robert Proctor summarizes his own review of this damning period in the history of evolutionary science as follows:

> What is slowly becoming clear is that scientists and physicians played a much greater role in the construction of Nazi policy than has heretofore been recognized; new efforts will no doubt continue to shed light on this darker, hidden chapter in the history of science.[21]

A Christian social and biological scientist, Dr. Jerry Bergman, has more recently published a most insightful and thoroughly documented study on "this darker chapter in the history of science." He summarized his findings and analysis as follows:

> A review of the writings of Hitler and contemporary German biologists finds that Darwin's theory and writings had a major influence on Nazi policies. . . . In the formation of his racial policies, [Hitler] relied heavily upon the Darwinian evolution model, especially the elaborations by Spencer and Haeckel. They culminated in the "final solution," the extermination of approximately six million Jews and four million other people who belonged to what German scientists judged were "inferior races."[22]

---

[19] George J. Stein, "Biological Science and Nazism," p. 53.
[20] Matt Cartmill, "Misdeeds in Anthropology," p. 858.
[21] Robert N. Proctor, "Science and Nazism," p. 731.
[22] Jerry Bergman, "Eugenics and the Development of Nazi Racial Policy," *Perspectives on Science and Christian Faith*, vol. 44 (June 1992), p. 109.

Racism and the Struggle for Life

Racism in perhaps its most virulent form came to fruition under Hitler and the Nazis in Germany in connection with World War II. However, racism in one form or another has been a part of human society all through history. Ever since Babel, when God separated the rebelling human populations into different nations and languages, there has been a sinful tendency for each national or tribal group to consider itself as either superior or inferior with respect to other groups, and this has led to what we call racism and racial conflicts.

This attitude is contrary to Scripture, of course, though there have been occasional attempts by some to find a pseudo-biblical rationale for it. The only supposed *scientific* rationale for racism, however, has been evolutionism, especially Darwinism. In fact, Darwin and Huxley and practically all the evolutionary scientists of the 19th century were doctrinaire racists, long before Hitler. As far as the Bible is concerned, the only "race" is the human race. Neither the word nor the concept of race is even mentioned at all in the Scriptures. "[God] hath made of one blood all nations of man for to dwell on all the face of the earth" (Acts 17:26). On the other hand, the subtitle of Darwin's *Origin of Species* was "The Preservation of Favored Races in the Struggle for Life."

The Germanic pride which led to the belief that the Teutonic Aryans were superior to other races was given a tremendous boost by Darwin's theories on "the preservation of favored races."

> Darwin's notion of struggle for survival was quickly appropriated by the racists . . . such struggle, legitimized by the latest scientific views, justified the racists' conception of superior and inferior peoples . . . and validated the struggle between them.[23]

It was not just in Germany, however, that scientific racism thrived. Darwin, Huxley, and others promoted such views in England, and the same was true of leading biologists and anthropologists in the United States, even well into the 20th century. The most influential American physical anthropologists (Osborn, Hooton, Hrdlicka, *et al.*) argued that the Caucasians were superior and the Africans inferior races.

Typical of prominent American biologists was the eminent Edwin G. Conklin, professor of biology at Princeton University, who said:

---

[23] Karl A. Schleunes, *The Twisted Road to Auschwitz* (Urbana, IL: University of Illinois Press, 1970), p. 30, 32. Cited by J. Bergman, "Eugenics and Nazi Racial Policy," p. 118.

> Comparison of any modern race with the Neanderthal or Heidelberg types show that . . . Negroid races more closely resemble the original stock than the white or yellow races. Every consideration should lead those who believe in the superiority of the white race to strive to preserve its purity and to establish and maintain the segregation of the races.[24]

This is not to say, of course, that modern evolutionists are all racists. It is no longer popular in America to be a racist, and liberals of every academic persuasion, including most (not all) modern evolutionary biologists decry and eschew racism.

This was not true of the 19th-century evolutionists, however. An important book has thoroughly reviewed this subject and demonstrated that literally *all* of the leading 19th-century evolutionists believed in the evolutionary superiority of the white race and the inferiority of the others, especially the Negro.[25] One reviewer said:

> This is an extremely important book, documenting as it does what has long been suspected: the ingrained, firm, and almost unanimous racism of North American men of science during the 19th (and into the 20th) century. . . . *Ab initio*, Afro-Americans were viewed by these intellectuals as being in certain ways unredeemably, unchangeably, irrevocably inferior.[26]

A reviewer in another scientific journal noted the following argument in the book:

> What was new in the Victorian period was Darwinism. . . . Before 1859, many scientists had questioned whether blacks were of the same species as whites. After 1859, the evolutionary schema raised additional questions, particularly whether or not Afro-Americans could survive competition with their white near-relations. The momentous answer was a resounding no. . . . The African was inferior because he represented the "missing link" between ape and Teuton.[27]

---

[24] Edwin G. Conklin, *The Direction of Human Evolution* (New York, NY: Scribner's, 1921), p. 34. Cited by Bergman, "Eugenics and Nazi Racial Policy," p. 115.

[25] John S. Haller, Jr., *Outcasts from Evolution: Scientific Attitudes of Racial Inferiority, 1859-1900* (Urbana, IL: University of Illinois Press, 1971).

[26] Sidney M. Mintz, *American Scientist*, vol. 60 (May/June 1972), p. 387.

[27] John C. Burham, *Science*, vol. 175 (February 4, 1972), p. 506.

With this kind of evolutionary thinking essentially universal, it is no wonder that the concepts of race were so important in the development of the master-race idea. Not only, however, were Hitler and others of his ilk ardent evolutionary racists, but so were Karl Marx and his socialist and communist colleagues, all on the basis of their evolutionary idealogies.

> On hearing this remark, the present writer asked the administrator whether this doctrine would not imply that the colonial, minority, and primitive peoples, those who had had less chance for mental and physical development, were not also genetically less advanced than the dominant ones. "Ah yes," he replied in confidential manner and after some hesitation, "yes, we must admit that this is, after all, true. They are in fact inferior to *us* biologically in every respect, including their heredity. And that," he added, "is in fact the official doctrine."[28]

For that matter, Charles Darwin himself was convinced of such assumed white superiority. Although he was opposed to slavery, he too thought that the Negro was of a backward race, and was doomed to become extinct in future evolutionary competition with the more favored races.

The very idea of "race," of course, was an evolutionary concept, not a biblical or Christian concept. To evolutionists, a race was essentially a sub-species, which, if isolated long enough, might well evolve into a new species, so the theory goes. Although most modern evolutionists hold to the monophyletic (single line), rather than polyphyletic origin of man, they do believe that the various races have been distinct for at least several score thousand years, so that ample time has been available to evolve significant differences between them. This possibility was mentioned even by such an ardent modern evolutionist as the late George Gaylord Simpson, who would, of course, have indignantly denied any charge of racism against himself.

> Evolution does not necessarily proceed at the same rate in different populations, so that among many groups of animals it is possible to find some species that have evolved more slowly, hence are now more primitive, as regards some particular trait or even overall. It is natural to ask —

[28] Conway Zirkle, *Evolution, Biology and the Social Scene* (Philadelphia, PA: University of Pennsylvania Press, 1959), p. 335.

> as many have asked — whether among human races there may not similarly be some that are more primitive in one way or another or in general. It is indeed possible to find single characteristics that are probably more advanced or more primitive in one race than in another.[29]

Now, of course, our whole point in this discussion is to show that, rightly or wrongly, evolutionary thinking is at the root of modern racism and racial conflicts. Once again, this is not meant at all to imply that all or even most modern evolutionists are themselves racists. It is just that evolution *itself* is fundamentally racist. As Sir Arthur Keith maintained:

> Christianity makes no distinction of race or of color; it seeks to break down all racial barriers. In this respect the hand of Christianity is against that of Nature, for are not the races of mankind the evolutionary harvest which Nature has toiled through long ages to produce? May we not say, then, that Christianity is anti-evolutionary in its aim? This may be a merit, but if so it is one which has not been openly acknowledged by Christian philosophers.[30]

The Bible, Evolution, and Modern Racism

Some people today, especially those of anti-Christian opinions, still have the mistaken notion that the Bible prescribes permanent racial divisions among men and is, therefore, the cause of modern racial hatreds. As a matter of fact, the Bible says nothing whatever about race. As far as one can learn from a study of Scripture, the writers of the Bible never referred to distinct races of men, in the sense of black and yellow and white races, or Caucasian and Mongol and Negroid races, or any other such divisions.

The biblical divisions among men are those of "tongues, families, nations, and lands," (Gen. 10:5, 20, 31) rather than races. The vision of the redeemed saints in heaven (Rev. 7:9) is one of "all nations, and kindreds, and people, and tongues," but no mention is made of "races." The formation of the original divisions, after the Flood, is based on different languages (Gen. 11:6, 9), supernaturally imposed by God, but nothing is said about any other physical differences.

Some have interpreted the Noahic prophecy concerning his three sons (Gen. 9:25-27) to refer to three races — Hamitic, Semitic, and

---

[29] George Gaylord Simpson, "The Biological Nature of Man," *Science*, vol. 152 (April 22, 1966), p. 475.

[30] Sir Arthur Keith, *Evolution and Ethics*, p. 72.

Japhetic — but such a meaning is in no way evident from the words of this passage. The prophecy applies to the descendants of Noah's sons, and the various nations to be formed from them, but nothing is said about three races. Modern anthropologists and historians have employed a much different terminology than this simple trifurcation (three-race division) for what they consider to be the various races among men.

Therefore, the origin of the concept of "race" must be sought elsewhere than in the Bible. If certain Christian writers have interpreted the Bible in a racist framework, the error is in the interpretation, not in the Bible itself. In the Bible, there is only one race — the human race!

In recent terminology, a race of men was thought to involve quite a large number of individual national and language groups. It was, therefore, a much broader generic concept than any of the biblical divisions. In the terminology of biological taxonomy, it was roughly the same as a "variety," or a "sub-species." Biologists, of course, use the term to apply to sub-species of animals, as well as men.

When Charles Darwin selected as the subtitle for his book the phrase "The Preservation of Favoured Races in the Struggle for Life," it was clear from the context that he had races of animals primarily in mind, but at the same time it is also clear, as we shall see, that he thought of races of men in the same way.

That this concept was still held until very recently is evident from the following words of leading modern evolutionist George Gaylord Simpson:

> Races of men have, or perhaps one should say "had," exactly the same biological significance as the sub-species of other species of mammals.[31]

It is evident, therefore, that a race is not a biblical category, but rather is a category of evolutionary biology. Each race is a sub-species, with a long evolutionary history of its own, supposedly in the process of evolving gradually into a distinct species.

One leading evolutionist suggests that each of the races has been around a long while.

> The simplest interpretation of this conclusion today would envision a relatively small group starting to spread not long after modern man appeared. With the spreading, groups became separated and isolated. Fifty thousand years or so is a short time in evolutionary terms, and this may

[31] George Gaylord Simpson, "The Biological Nature of Man," p. 474.

help to explain why, genetically speaking, human races show relatively small differences.[32]

As applied to man, this concept, of course, suggests that each of the various races of men is very different (though still interfertile) from all of the others. If they continue to be segregated, each will continue to compete as best it can with the other races in the struggle for existence, and finally the fittest will survive. Or else, perhaps, they will gradually become so different from each other as to assume the character of separate species altogether (just as apes and men *supposedly* diverged from a common ancestor in the so-called Tertiary Period).

Most modern biologists today would express these concepts somewhat differently than as above, and they undoubtedly would disavow the racist connotations. Nevertheless, this was certainly the point of view of the 19th century evolutionists, and it is difficult to interpret modern evolutionary theory, at least the so-called neo-Darwinian synthesis, much differently.

The rise of evolutionary theory took place mostly in Europe, especially in England and Germany. Europeans, along with their American cousins, were then leading the world in industrial and military expansion, and were, therefore, inclined to think of themselves as somehow superior to the other nations of the world. This opinion was tremendously encouraged by the concurrent rise of Darwinian evolutionism and its simplistic approach to the idea of struggle between natural races, with the only strongest surviving and thus contributing to the advance of evolution.

As the 19th century scientists were converted to evolution, they were thus also convinced of racism. They were certain that the white race was superior to other races, and the reason for this superiority was to be found in Darwinian theory. The white race had advanced further up the evolutionary ladder and, therefore, was destined either to eliminate the other races in the struggle for existence or else to have to assume the "white man's burden" and to care for those inferior races that were incompetent to survive otherwise.

Charles Darwin himself, though strongly opposed to slavery on moral grounds, was convinced of white racial superiority. He wrote on one occasion as follows:

> I could show fight on natural selection having done and doing more for the progress of civilization than you seem

[32] L. L. Cavalli-Sforza, "The Genetics of Human Populations," *Scientific American*, vol. 231 (September 1974), p. 89.

> inclined to admit. . . . The more civilized so-called Caucasian races have beaten the Turkish hollow in the struggle for existence. Looking to the world at no very distant date, what an endless number of the lower races will have been eliminated by the higher civilized races throughout the world.[33]

The man more responsible than any other for the widespread acceptance of evolution in the 19th century was Thomas Huxley. Soon after the American Civil War, in which the Negro slaves were freed, he wrote as follows:

> No rational man, cognizant of the facts, believes that the average Negro is the equal, still less the superior, of the white man. And if this be true, it is simply incredible that, when all his disabilities are removed, and our prognathous relative has a fair field and no favour, as well as no oppressor, he will be able to compete successfully with his bigger-brained and smaller-jawed rival, in a contest which is to be carried out by thoughts and not by bites.[34]

Racist sentiments such as these were held by all the 19th century evolutionists, as shown by Haller in the book mentioned previously.

In a day and age that practically worshipped at the shrine of scientific progress, as was true especially during the century from 1860 to 1960, such universal scientific racism was bound to have repercussions in the political and social realms. The seeds of evolutionary racism came to fullest fruition in the form of National Socialism in Germany. The philosopher Friedrich Nietzsche, a contemporary of Charles Darwin and an ardent evolutionist himself, popularized in Germany his concept of the superman, and then the master race. The ultimate outcome was Hitler, who elevated this savage philosophy to the status of a national policy.

In recent decades, the cause of racial liberation has made racism unpopular with intellectuals and only a few evolutionary scientists still openly espouse the idea of a long-term polyphyletic origin of the different races.[35] On the other hand, in recent years, the pendulum has

---

[33] Charles Darwin, *Life and Letters, 1*, letter to W. Graham, July 3, 1881, p. 316; cited in *Darwin and the Darwinian Revolution*, by Gertrude Himmelfarb (London: Chatto and Windus, 1959), p. 343.

[34] Thomas Huxley, *Lay Sermons, Addresses and Reviews* (New York, NY: Appleton, 1871), p. 20.

[35] One notable exception, among others, was the leading anthropologist Carleton Coon. See *The Origin of Races* (New York, NY: Alfred Knopf, 1962).

swung, and we have had highly vocal advocates of "black power" and "red power" and "yellow power," and these advocates are all doctrinaire evolutionists also, who believe their own respective "races" are the fittest to survive in man's continuing struggle for existence.

According to the biblical record of history, however, the Creator's divisions among men are linguistic and national divisions, *not racial*. Each nation has a distinct purpose and function in the corporate life of mankind, in the divine plan (as, for that matter, does each person).

> [God] hath made of one blood, all nations of men for to dwell on all the face of the earth, and hath determined the times before appointed, and the bounds of their habitation; That they should seek the Lord, if haply they might feel after Him, and find Him (Acts 17:26-27).

No one nation is "better" than another, except in the sense of the blessings that it has received from the Creator, perhaps in measure of its obedience to His Word and fulfillment of its calling. Such blessings are not an occasion for pride, but for gratitude.

The Racism of Darwinism

The fact that Darwinian evolution is the basis of modern racism is finally being acknowledged — and even emphasized — by many modern evolutionists, after being indignantly denied for so long by older evolutionists whenever creationists would mention it. Stephen Jay Gould says, for example, speaking of the now-discredited recapitulation theory, which was long used as an argument for evolution:

> This theory, often expressed by the mouthful "ontogeny recapitulates phylogeny," held that higher animals, in their embryonic development, pass through a series of stages representing, in proper sequence, the adult forms of ancestral, lower creatures. . . . Recapitulation provided a convenient focus for the pervasive racism of white scientists.[36]

Gould rightly pointed out that this absurd theory is now defunct, as it should be, but the strange thing is that many people still believe it. Any

---

[36] Stephen Jay Gould, "Dr. Down's Syndrome," *Natural History*, vol. 89, April 1980), p. 144. The title of this article has reference to the physiologic infirmity widely known as mongolism, first described and named by Dr. Down. The idea was that the "races" had evolved as Negroid, Mongoloid, and Caucasoid, in that order, and that a mongoloid child, in his embryologic and infantile growth, had simply been arrested at that stage in his evolutionary recapitulation.

lingering doubt should have been eliminated by modern fetoscopy, which can actually monitor the fetal growth in the womb.

> Fetoscopy makes it possible to observe directly the unborn child through a tiny telescope inserted through the uterine wall. . . . The development of the child — from the union of the partners' cells to birth — has been studied exhaustively. As a result, long-held beliefs have been put to rest. We now know, for instance, that man, in his prenatal stages, does not go through the complete evolution of life — from a primitive single cell to a fish-like creature to man. Today it is known that every step in the fetal developmental process is specifically human.[37]

Nevertheless, as Gould said, this theory did provide in the 19th century "the best guide for the organization of life into sequences of higher and lower forms." It was *not* the stratigraphic sequences, but the recapitulation theory popularized by Ernst Haeckel and the Great Chain of Being concept that gave 19th century paleontologists a system for organizing their fossils into an evolutionary series.

That the profound racism engendered by such notions persisted well into the 20th century was demonstrated in a remarkable article by Henry Fairfield Osborn, probably the leading evolutionary anthropologist of the first half of the 20th century, as well as president of the American Museum of Natural History.

> If an unbiased zoologist were to descend upon the earth from Mars and study the races of man with the same impartiality as the races of fishes, birds, and mammals, he would undoubtedly divide the existing races of man into several genera and into a very large number of species and sub-species.[38]

Note the evolutionary use of the term "race" here, a word (or concept) which never appears in the Bible, despite the specious contention of some evolutionists that racism is derived from a fundamentalist interpretation of Scripture. Osborn then continues:

> This is the recognition that the genus *Homo* is subdivided into three absolutely distinct stocks, which in zool-

---

[37] Sabine Schwabenthan, "Life Before Birth," *Parents* (October 1979), p. 50.

[38] Henry Fairfield Osborn, "The Evolution of Human Races," *Natural History* (January/February 1926), reprinted in *Natural History,* vol. 89 (April 1980), p. 129.

> ogy would be given the rank of species, if not of genera, stocks popularly known as the Caucasian, the Mongolian, and the Negroid.
>
> The spiritual, intellectual, moral, and physical characters which separate these three great human stocks are far more profound and ancient than those which divide the Nordic, Alpine, and Mediterranean races. In my opinion, these three primary stocks diverged from each other before the beginning of the Pleistocene or Ice Age. . . . The standard of intelligence of the average adult Negro is similar to that of the eleven-year-old youth of the species *Homo sapiens*.[39]

Such scientifically flawed thinking reveals personal bigotry, and has led to much human misery. Thankfully, it is no longer prominent, although recently on the rise again. Modern punctuational evolutionists such as Gould have made their point that Darwinism has led to racism. They have also stressed its culpability with respect to social Darwinism (exploitative capitalism, imperialism, etc.), but this has long been acknowledged, with regrets, even by neo-Darwinists. They are not so eager to acknowledge its responsibility for Fascism and Nazism (after all, Mussolini and Hitler *did* call their movements "socialistic," and the student movements of the 1960s bore many striking resemblances to the Hitler youth of the 1930s and early 1940s), but the connection is certainly there, as we have already shown.

> Hitler believed in struggle as a Darwinian principle of human life that forced every people to try to dominate all others; without struggle they would rot and perish. . . . Even in his defeat in April 1945 Hitler expressed his faith in the survival of the stronger and declared the Slavic peoples to have proved themselves the stronger.[40]

James Ferguson has also recently reminded us that the quasi-scientific evolutionary racism of the 19th century had a deadly impact on the world.

> In 19th century Europe the concept of race was a preoccupation for the growing human sciences. . . . These first physical anthropologists helped to develop the concept of Aryan supremacy, which later fueled the institu-

---

[39] *Ibid.*

[40] P. Hoffman, *Hitler's Personal Security* (London: Pergamon Press, 1979), p. 264.

> tional racism of Germany in the 1930s, and of South Africa today.[41]

Similarly, Stephen Jay Gould in another significant article has noted that evolutionary anthropologists were long convinced that the various "races" all had separate evolutionary origins and, therefore, had "evolved" to different levels of intelligence and ability during their long histories.

> We cannot understand much of the history of late 19th and early 20th century anthropology, with its plethora of taxonomic names proposed for nearly every scrap of fossil bone, unless we appreciate its obsession with the identification and ranking of races.[42]

And, since these anthropologists all were white Europeans or Americans, they were confident that the Caucasian race had advanced far above the "lower" races. Gould himself rejects racism, however, on the shaky grounds that human separation into racial subdivisions is too "recent" for significant differences to have developed:

> The division of humans into modern "racial" groups is a product of our recent history. It does not predate the origin of our own species, *Homo sapiens*, and probably occurred during the last few tens (or at most hundreds) of thousands of years.[43]

Dr. Gould, however, seems to be arguing against himself here. If the "races" have been segregated for possibly a "few hundreds of thousands of years," then it is completely arbitrary to assume that no significant racial differences would evolve in such immense spans of time — that is, if evolution were really true. Gould's own concept of punctuated equilibrium involves evolutionary "jerks," which produce significant evolutionary changes in only a few generations. Evolutionism — whether the slow and gradual changes of new-Darwinism or the rapid jumps of punctuationism — is, by its very nature, racist in its implications!

In contrast, biblical creationism, with its record of the *recent* origin of all the tribes and nations after the great Flood, only a few thousand

---

[41] James Ferguson, "The Laboratory of Racism," *New Scientist*, vol. 103 (September 27, 1984), p. 18.

[42] Stephen Jay Gould, "Human Equality is a Contingent Fact of History," *Natural History*, vol. 93 (November 1984), p. 28.

[43] *Ibid.*, p. 31.

years ago, makes real "races," in the evolutionary sense, quite impossible. This fact, of course, correlates perfectly with the biblical teaching that there is only one race — the human race!

As noted before, the very idea of "race" is strictly an evolutionary concept, though it did not originate with Darwin. Darwin appropriated it from previous evolutionists. As far as the Bible is concerned, all people are of "one blood," descended from Noah and his three sons in only a few thousand years, not nearly enough to develop real races in the evolutionary sense (that is, sub-species in the process of evolving into new species).

This also is a fact not known or appreciated by most Christians. All the tensions and tragedies of racial conflicts stem from racist philosophy, which is squarely based on an evolutionary view of human origins and history. R. W. Wrangham, reviewing this subject, has said:

> Even if particular individuals from different populations occasionally look alike, surely the distinctions between whole populations are big enough to justify calling them racial. This was the dominant view from the mid-18th century onward. . . . Authors varied in their opinion of the number of human races, from Cuvier's three to as many as thirty or more in the 20th century, but with few exceptions they agreed that the concept of race was sound.[44]

Similarly, anthropologist Russell Tuttle, of the University of Chicago, in reviewing an article by Loring Brace, says:

> Brace squarely confronts racist influences in the two chief founders of institutional physical anthropology in the United States . . . [Ales] Hrdlicka, based at the American Museum of Natural History, and E. A. Hooton, with whom most of the second generation of physical anthropologists studied at Harvard.[45]

Dr. Brace (with whom one of us once had a creation/evolution debate) was, like Tuttle, a leading modern evolutionary anthropologist, at the University of Michigan. Hrdlicka and Hooton, along with Henry Fairfield Osborne, also at the American Museum of Natural History, were leading American anthropologists of the first half of the 20th century, and all were scientific racists, as Tuttle says. In fact, as noted

---

[44] R. W. Wrangham, Book Review, *American Scientist*, vol. 72 (Jan./Feb. 1984), p. 75.
[45] Russell Tuttle, "Five Decades of Anthropology," *Science*, vol. 220 (1982), p. 832.

previously, Osborne even taught that the Negro "race" was actually a lower species than *Homo sapiens*!

However, the current generation of anthropologists, largely because of anti-racist pressures from the liberal and Marxist "left-wing" of evolutionary thought, are finally beginning to abandon the ideas of race altogether, and thus are inadvertently returning to the biblical concept. Tuttle puts it this way:

> [Brace] reiterates the modern view that we should abandon the concept of race altogether and instead record the gene frequencies and traits of populations that are identified simply by their geographic localities. This genotypic and phenotypic information is to be interpreted in terms of historical and proximate selective forces.[46]

R. W. Wrangham, who is on the staff of the Center for Advanced Study in the Behavioral Sciences at Stanford University, says: "The dominant view today is that race is an outmoded concept."[47] Similarly, Gould says that: "Human variation exists; the formal designation of the races is passé."[48]

For whatever it's worth, the senior writer of this book has been teaching and writing almost the same thing about the race concept for over 50 years, at least 25 years in advance of the modern school of anthropologists. This was not because of his personal knowledge of human genetics, which was minimal at best, but simply because this was the teaching of Scripture.

Thus, racism has depended on evolutionism for its pseudo-scientific promotion, especially Darwinism and neo-Darwinian evolutionism. Consequently, evolutionary thinking has been an integral component of social Darwinism, imperialism, and, finally, fascism and Nazism, as well as a basic underlying cause of both World War I and World War II.

This brings us to perhaps an even more important and more deadly socio-economic philosophy — that is, Marxism, with its associated Socialistic, Communistic, and anarchistic branches. This philosophy also was squarely grounded on evolutionism, though perhaps more aligned with Lamarckianism or (more recently) punctuationism, than with neo-Darwinism.

---

46 Russell Tuttle, "Five Decades of Anthropology," *Science*, vol. 220 (1982), p. 832.

47 R. W. Wrangham, *American Scientist*, p. 75.

48 S. J. Gould, "Human Equality," p. 30.

Revolutionary Evolutionism and Communism

It is well known that Communism, as practiced in the Soviet Union, Red China, Vietnam, Castroite Cuba, and other nations where it has flourished for a time, was founded on the atheistic premises of Marx, Lenin, and other Communist leaders. The supposed scientific basis of Marxism was evolutionism, though the particular form of evolutionism (Lamarckianism, Darwinism, punctuationism, pantheism) has varied with circumstances.

Marxist theory not only was based on atheism, but also urged the complete destruction of religion, especially Christianity. Religion was "the opiate of the people," so they said, while desecrating churches and slaughtering or enslaving Christians who would not renounce their faith and, in effect, worship the state. Lenin expressed his anti-theism thus:

> Every religious idea of a god, even flirting with the idea of god, is unutterable vileness of the most dangerous kind, "contagion" of the most abominable kind. Millions of sins, filthy deeds, acts of violence, and physical contagions are far less dangerous *than the subtle spiritual idea of a god.*[49]

This premise, of course, not only denigrated religion, but also meant that individual men and women, being merely animals, were quite expendable if their elimination would serve the interests of "the people" as a whole (or, more realistically, the intellectual elite who had attained rule over the people as a whole).

> The problem is that, by denying the possibility of a relationship between God and man, atheism also denies the possibility of a just relationship between men. . . . Human life is sacred only if there is a God to sanctify it. Otherwise man is just another collection of atoms and can be treated as such. . . . The spiritual disorder within man's soul of which Saint James wrote has become, in the modern age, institutionalized. In other words, the moral disorder of the individual soul has become the principle of a general public disorder, first as it was articulated in the teachings of Nietzsche and Marx, and then incarnated in the Nazi regime and in the various Marxist-Leninist states today.[50]

[49] Vladimer Lenin, as cited in "Atheism and Arms Control," by Robert R. Reilly, *Intercollegiate Review*, vol. 24 (Fall 1988), p. 20. Emphasis his.

[50] Robert R. Reilly, *Intercollegiate Review,* p. 19.

The writings of Karl Marx have spawned a variety of liberal panaceas in the world, including various socialist schemes as well as doctrinaire communism. Even today, with Communism as practiced in Russia and eastern Europe somewhat defeated and dispersed, the teachings of Marx continue to thrive in China, Vietnam, and many other places, including many universities in western Europe, South America, and even the United States. And all are grounded in evolutionism!

> All manner of liberal thinkers have appropriated Darwin to find at last a scientific foundation for the liberal belief in progress, democratic equalitarian socialism, and an altruistic ethic of human solidarity. Marx himself viewed Darwin's work as confirmation by the natural sciences of his own views, and even Mao Tse-tung regarded Darwin as presented by the German Darwinists, as the foundation of Chinese scientific socialism.[51]

In the early days of Russian Communism, after its harsh control over Russian society had been firmly established, Russian scientists were expected to promote evolutionism, and they did. The Russian biochemist Oparin, an ardent Marxist, was the one man most instrumental in establishing the modern dogma of the naturalistic origin of life, the view which (despite the utter lack of any scientific proof) is now almost universally taught and believed, even in the high schools of America.

As Michael Ruse, an ardent Darwinist opponent of the Marxist influence on American evolutionary thought, although himself a believer in the biochemical origin of life, has pointed out:

> [Oparin] was quite open in his subscription to a Marxist-Leninist philosophy of nature, and consciously applied it to his work on the appearance of new life.[52]

Which brings us, then, to a consideration of evolution as it was understood by the communists, the Russians in particular, for it is *this* model which seems to have captivated the hearts of the modern school of western evolutionists.

Karl Marx, of course, was a committed evolutionist *before* Darwin published *The Origin of Species*, but he was such because of his atheistic

---

[51] George J. Stein, "Biological Science and the Roots of Nazism," *American Scientist*, vol. 76 (January/February 1988), p. 52.

[52] Michael Ruse, "Biology and Values: A Fresh Look," in Barcun Marcus et al., *Logic Methodology and Philosophy of Science* (New York, NY: Elsevier Science Publications B.V., 1986), p. 456.

faith (born a Jew, he had once made a Christian confession, presumably for economic reasons, but later renounced all organized religions in favor of atheism) and his commitment to change in human history and economic systems, but he had no real scientific basis for this secular faith until Darwin came along. As is well known, Marx even wanted to dedicate *Das Kapital* to Darwin, but Darwin refused.

In spite of Marxist commitment to evolution, however, both Marx himself and later communists were always uncomfortable with the uniformitarian aspects of Darwinism. They honored Darwin because of the scientific respectability that he had given to naturalism and atheism, but they needed a more immediate mechanism for evolutionary change than the ideas of long-drawn-out progress which commended themselves to western Europe and America, the nations of which were experiencing unprecedented growth and development.

Lamarckianism was very appealing to the Communist mind, for it promised evolution through changing the environment. This could be a considerably more rapid process than the cut-and-try mechanism of natural selection. A revolutionary change imposed on the environment could produce all sorts of physical, as well as social, benefits to society, through the Lamarckian inheritability of characters produced environmentally. For a considerable time, therefore, this concept was even imposed on Russian scientists as official state dogma.

The problem, of course, was that Lamarckian evolution — unlike Darwinian conjectures and tautologies — was testable! It was, indeed, subjected to many scientific experiments, and, in spite of optimistic claims made for awhile by such Russian scientists as Kammerer, Pavlov, Lysenko, and others, it was eventually so completely falsified by tests that Lamarckianism finally had to be officially repudiated.

This did not mean, however, that Russian scientism would simply capitulate to neo-Darwinism, for this was the quasi-official dogma of western capitalism, and, besides, it acted too slowly. Communism must proceed by *revolution*, not by slow-and-gradual *evolution*! To be scientific, some form of naturalistic mechanism had to be found that would elevate systems rapidly — not gradually — to a higher state. And so, apparently, was born the complex of concepts which we have called *revolutionary evolutionism*.

Steven Stanley describes the introduction of this system of evolutionary thought to North America as follows:

> The punctuational idea emerged as a more visible alternative to English-speaking paleontologists with the

> publication of Eldredge (1971) and Eldredge and Gould (1972). It is both interesting and surprising that, unknown to Americans, this view had previously gained support in the paleontologic community of the Soviet Union.[53]

Stephen J. Gould and Niles Eldredge have themselves admitted this Marxist pedigree for their theory. First, however, they present this philosophical justification:

> Alternative conceptions of change have respectable pedigrees in philosophy. Hegel's dialectical laws, translated into a materialist context, have become the official "state philosophy" of many socialist nations. These laws of change are explicitly punctuational, as befits a theory of revolutionary transformation in human society.[54]

These authors thus stress that Hegel's dialectical materialism, which was adopted by Marx as communist dogma, when put in the context of materialistic evolution is the state "philosophy" (read "state religion") of those nations that became communist (or "socialist").

Another geologist seemingly sympathetic to Marxist "science" has commented similarly, as follows:

> The theory of dialectic materialism postulates matter as the ultimate reality, not to be questioned. . . . Evolution is more than a useful biologic concept: it is a natural law controlling the history of all phenomena.[55]

That author, J. E. O'Rourke, proceeds to justify the use of circular reasoning in geologic dating and other interpretations, denying any real significance to so-called "absolute time" (so important in uniformitarian neo-Darwinism) on the basis of this materialistic premise, saying in effect that all that counts is pragmatism — that is, whether a system works out or not.

Gould and Eldredge apparently believe that Marxist philosophy will work and are quite pleased to be able to replace the capitalistic system of evolution with the Marxist brand.

---

[53] Steven M. Stanley, *Macroevolution: Pattern and Process* (San Francisco, CA: W. H. Freeman and Co., 1979), p. 36.

[54] Stephen J. Gould and Niles Eldredge, "Punctuated Equilibria: The Tempo and Mode of Evolution Reconsidered," *Paleobiology*, vol. 3 (Spring 1977), p. 145.

[55] J. E. O'Rourke, "Pragmatism versus Materialism in Stratigraphy," *American Journal of Science*, vol. 276 (January 1976), p. 51.

> In the light of this official philosophy, it is not at all surprising that a punctuational view of speciation, much like our own, but devoid (so far as we can tell) of references to synthetic evolutionary theory and the allopatric model, has long been favored by many Russian paleontologists. It may also not be irrelevant to our personal preferences that one of us learned his Marxism, literally, at his daddy's knee.[56]

Interestingly, Gould has occasionally been embarrassed by his Marxist reputation and has waffled about it somewhat. On other occasions, however (at least once when under oath), he has acknowledged that he is, indeed, a Marxist, and he is generally recognized as such by his colleagues (there are many other Marxists in the American academic world today, especially at Harvard, M.I.T., and other "prestige" schools). A recent reference to Gould in the "theoretical and discussion journal of the British Communist Party" says, however, that he is *not* a Marxist.

> The most eloquent defender of scientific evolutionism, Stephen Jay Gould, is an avowedly non-Marxist radical — on the left of the scientific/political consensus, but working well and truly within it.[57]

It would, no doubt, in the current situation, serve the interests of doctrinaire Marxism best for such a prominent scientific evolutionist as Gould *not* to be identified officially as a Marxist, whatever his actual beliefs may be. This article also has the following to say about evolution in general:

> Aspects of evolutionism are perfectly consistent with Marxism. The explanation of the origins of humankind and of mind by purely natural forces was, and remains, as welcome to Marxists as to any other secularists. The sources of value and responsibility are not to be found in a separate mental realm or in an immortal soul, much less in the inspired words of the Bible.[58]

In any case, the introduction of punctuationism into American evolutionary thinking just two decades ago has rolled almost like a tidal wave over the whole field, especially the younger generation of evolutionists, disenamored with the capitalistic establishment and seeking

[56] Gould and Eldredge, "Punctuated Equilibria," p. 146.
[57] Robert M. Young, "The Darwin Debate," *Marxism Today*, vol. 26 (April 1982), p. 22.
[58] *Ibid.*, p. 21.

social justice and full egalitarianism not by slow evolutionary change, but by rapid and even violent change if need be! Gould and his colleagues have been lionized as leaders of this new wave of revolutionary science. Gould (as well as Carl Sagan, Carl Johanson, and other young evolutionists) are personable, intelligent, articulate, and extremely popular. Gould has been featured on the cover of *Newsweek*, named "Man-of-the-Year in Science" by *Discover*, has appeared as guest star on the "Donahue Show" and other national telecasts, and has received great adulation. Sagan (with his super-expensive *Cosmos* series on the Public Broadcasting System), Johanson (with his famous "Lucy" hominid — named after a spaced-out character in a Beatle's song), and others have received almost as much notoriety as Gould in the feverish promotion of evolutionism by the news media in recent years.

Stephen Jay Gould is the generally acknowledged leader of this new style of evolutionism. In fact, he is probably the most articulate and influential evolutionist in today's world. With the current decline of Communism as a world power base, he has either altered his Marxist convictions or at least is keeping them more to himself. However, as Michael Ruse has pointed out, his basic punctuationist view of evolutionary history clearly has its roots in his (perhaps former) Marxist philosophy.

> Much of Gould's justification for his paleontological perspective comes from Marxist philosophy. . . . Gould criticized Darwinian gradualism as being just an act of faith, reflecting Darwin's own 19th century liberal views about the virtues of gradual (as opposed to revolutionary) change. Gould, to the contrary, endorses a view which leads him to expect rapid, abrupt breaks with the past. His view of the fossil record is therefore simply his own world picture made, if not flesh, then stone.[59]

In a sense, Gould is a product of the youth rebellion of the sixties. One remarkable spin-off was the development of a strong reaction against the older generation of scientists, as well as against the older generation in general. This meant, among other things, rebellion against the Darwinist doctrine of slow-and-gradual evolution in biology and against the Lyellian doctrine of uniformitarianism in geology, with the recent graduates in these fields preaching and promoting "quantum

---

59 Michael Ruse, "Biology and Values: A Fresh Look," in Barcun Marcus et al., *Logic Methodology and Philosophy of Science* (New York, NY: Elsevier Science Publications B.V., 1986), p. 460.

speciation" or "punctuated evolution" in biology, and "catastrophism" and "extinctionism" in geology.

This development was partly because these younger evolutionists had recognized the *complete absence* of scientific evidence for Darwinian-type evolution which creationists had been emphasizing for so long. But it was also because the social implications of traditional Darwinism (social Darwinism, racism, Nazism, imperialism, laissez-faire capitalism) were now being repudiated in the name of left-wing evolutionism (Marxism, communism, revolutionism). Commenting on these changes as they spilled over into the field of physical anthropology, Matt Cartmill makes this observation:

> When people turn indignantly from one sort of speculation to embrace another, there are usually good, non-scientific reasons for it. . . . A myth, says my dictionary, is a real fictional story that embodies the cultural ideals of a people or expresses deep, commonly felt emotions. By this definition, myths are generally good things — and the origin stories that paleoanthropologists tell are necessarily myths.[60]

This recent conflict between the slow-and-gradual (Darwinian) evolutionists and the "punctuationist," revolutionary evolutionists, with its overtones of the classic conflict between the older generation and the younger generation, as well as of that between traditional "social-Darwinist," laissez-faire, capitalistic economics and environmentalist (neo-Lamarckian), neo-catastrophist, Marxist economics, has been quite bitter, especially in England and the United States.

The American controversy focused especially at Harvard University, where two of today's leading evolutionists, Dr. Stephen Jay Gould and Dr. Edward O. Wilson, squared off as the spokesmen for these two opposing schools of evolutionary thought. Gould is the chief American spokesman for "punctuated equilibrium," and Wilson for "sociobiology," the modern equivalent of traditional neo-Darwinism. Reporting on this conflict, Dr. John Turner, reader in evolutionary genetics at the University of Leeds in England, says in a review article on this situation:

> It was the turn of E. O. Wilson and Richard Dawkins to be denounced, not this time from the pulpit as atheists, but by radical movements as fascist sympathizers. A

[60] Matt Cartmill, *Natural History*, vol. 92 (November 1983), p. 77.

Harvard group denounced Wilson's work as being in the intellectual tradition of Adolph Hitler.[61]

Richard Dawkins is well known in England as the Oxford professor who originated the "selfish gene" theory and the "blind watchmaker" euphemism for Darwinism. With reference to Gould, Turner continues with this identification:

> Stephen Gould, who has repeatedly urged the need to see man as essentially different from animals, and was one of the signatories of the "Hitler" statement about E. O. Wilson, has found the answer in the punctuated equilibrium theory.[62]

Now, Wilson and Dawkins both vigorously deny any connection with Nazism, as do their followers, but there can be little doubt that, if they were alive today, Hitler and Himmler and the Nazi theoreticians would appropriate their sociobiological arguments as further scientific support for their Nazi racist and survival-of-the-fittest philosophies. Dawkins and Wilson, of course, are both doctrinaire atheists, although Wilson testifies that he was once a Southern Baptist fundamentalist before encountering evolutionary teachings as a student at the University of Alabama.[63]

Gould and his many followers may, as Turner says, view man as distinct from animals, but this is in a Marxist sense, not in a biblical or creationist perspective. That is, *Homo sapiens* is believed to have appeared suddenly — not by creation, but by an evolutionary jerk, as Turner calls it. Gould is as much an atheist as Wilson or Dawkins. In fact, as noted above, he has admitted to being a Marxist, not a card-carrying communist, but someone committed to the philosophy and teachings of Karl Marx, which include atheism and evolutionism as foundational.

In commenting further on this latter-day conflict between these two schools of evolutionary atheism, Turner makes the interesting admission that *neither* is based on good scientific evidence.

> Of the essential jerk theory, one can say as Gould did of sociobiology, that it brings no new insights, and can cite on its behalf not a single unambiguous fact.
>
> The point is not that the punctuated equilibrium

---

61 John Turner, "Why We Need Evolution by Jerks," *New Scientist*, vol. 101 (February 9, 1984), p. 34.

62 *Ibid.*, p. 35.

63 E. O. Wilson, "Toward a Humanistic Biology," *The Humanist* (October 1982), p. 40.

> theory is wrong. It might be right. The point is that despite its very poor scientific foundations it is attracting an enormous amount of attention. And as the Harvard radicals so cogently argued in the case of race and IQ, when an essentially meretricious scientific theory causes such a fuss, we must look to non-scientific causes.[64]

That is, both the neo-Darwinists (including sociobiologists) and the punctuationists (reflecting their Marxist tendencies) hold their views for non-scientific reasons! Once again, as we have been stressing in this book, *evolution is not science; it is always religion* in one form or another.

As bitterly opposed as they are to each other, all the sects of evolutionism unite when confronted with creationism, their common enemy. And they especially hate *scientific* creationism, even though they must realize that they have no valid scientific proof or even good evidence for either slow evolution or sudden evolution. As bitter enemies of the true God and biblical Christianity, they prefer anything — any lie — to the truth of creation.

Now, commitment to evolution is nothing new for Marxism — whether the philosophical Marxism of the textbooks or the violent communism of the revolutionaries. All Socialists, Communists, anarchists, Leninists, Stalinists, Trotskyites, Maoists, Castroites, or whatever a particular school of Marxism or a particular Marxist national revolutionary movement may be called locally — all are founded upon evolutionism (whether Darwinian, Lamarckian, or some other brand) and atheism (even when it is called humanism or pantheism or something else).

It is time — high time, late time — for Christians to become alert to the fact that creationism is the only real antidote to this left-wing ideology that in one form enslaved more than half the world and is now almost at our own gates in another form. It may not conquer the free world by revolution and military power; but even our own schools and other public institutions, by its intellectual pretensions, are all based on its atheistic, evolutionary, pseudo-scientific presuppositions.

Creationists are frequently criticized for saying that evolutionism is not merely a scientific concept but that it also has been the basis of anti-Christian social systems such as communism and socialism. Critics of creationism often express indignation when such charges are made against evolutionary theory.

[64] Turner, "Why We Need Evolution by Jerks," p. 35.

No creationist, of course, ever alleges that all evolutionists are atheists or communists. There are multitudes of both theistic evolutionists and evolutionary capitalists. However, it is a simple fact that evolutionary thinking is basic in Socialism and Communism and other such systems, whatever conclusion one wishes to draw from that fact. Socialistic and Communistic writers frequently make a point of this, maintaining that the evolutionary structure proves their system to be "scientific."

For example, the famous periodical *International Socialist Review* (which includes a monthly supplement called its "Monthly Magazine Supplement to the Militant"), in its November 1980 issue, had as its feature article a lengthy attack on creationism entitled "Evolution vs. Creationism: In Defense of Scientific Thinking," by Cliff Conner. Although the author exhibits only a very limited knowledge of creationist arguments and cites no creationist publication, he does attempt a rather sketchy summary of evidences for evolution (including the long-discredited recapitulation theory!).

Of particular interest, however, is his concern that the creation movement may retard the advance of Marxism and Socialism. Conner stresses the importance of evolution to these systems in such assertions as the following:

> Defending Darwin is nothing new for socialists. The socialist movement recognized Darwinism as an important element in its general world outlook right from the start. When Darwin published his *Origin of Species* in 1859, Karl Marx wrote a letter to Frederick Engels in which he said: "This is the book which contains the basis in natural history for our view."
>
> By defending Darwinism, working people strengthen their defenses against the attacks of these reactionary outfits, and prepare the way for the transformation of the social order.[65]

Conner identifies himself and his colleagues as "revolutionary socialists," whose aim is "as Marx said: not merely to interpret the world but to change it."

The article concludes with an adulational testimony to Darwin.

> And of all those eminent researchers of the 19th

[65] Cliff Conner, "Evolution versus Creationism: In Defense of Scientific Thinking," *International Socialist Review: Monthly Magazine Supplement to the Militant* (November 1980).

> century who have left us such a rich heritage of knowledge, we are especially grateful to Charles Darwin for opening our way to an evolutionary dialectical understanding of nature.[66]

We suggest as biblical creationists, therefore, that those theistic evolutionists and evolutionary capitalists who attack creationists for suggesting an affinity between evolutionism and socialism should concentrate, instead, on attacking Marxists for suggesting this same affinity! They started it!

We particularly need to be alert to the fact that the modern shift by evolutionists to punctuated equilibrium and catastrophism is not a move toward biblical creationism and flood geology, as some might have hoped. If anything, it is even more inimical (as a closer counterfeit) to true creationism than was the old-style evolutionary uniformitarianism. This new system is nothing less than a very dangerous conditioning for revolution.

The older style Darwinian evolution, postulating the slow and gradual development of new species over millions of years, is rapidly being displaced by the idea that evolution proceeds in sudden jumps or revolutions. This theory of "punctuated equilibrium," introduced in 1972 and vigorously promoted by a vocal group of younger evolutionists under Gould's leadership is rapidly taking over the universities and colleges — even high schools!

The similarity of this type of evolutionary theory to Marxian revolutionary theory, which advocates social and economic evolution by intervals of intense revolution, is more than coincidental. The well-known gaps in the so-called fossil record, which actually give strong support to the special creation of each basic kind of organism, have been distorted to teach catastrophic evolution instead, and this concept in turn is used to support Marxist concepts of social change. This evaluation is confirmed by one of England's leading evolutionists, Professor L. B. Halstead, who is himself (like Gould) an atheist, but who still believes in slow and gradual evolution. Writing in the leading science journal, *Nature*, he observes:

> This presents the public for the first time with the notion that there are no actual fossils directly antecedent to man . . . [as] . . . the creationists have insisted on for years.[67]

---

[66] *Ibid.*

[67] L. B. Halstead, "Museum of Errors," *Nature* (November 20, 1980), p. 280.

Halstead charges that these "saltatory [jumping] evolutionists" are politically motivated, and he calls their theory "the recipe for revolution." He then makes an unexpected comparison:

> Just as there are "scientific" creationists seeking to falsify the concept of gradual change through time in favor of catastrophism, so too there are the Marxists who for different motives are equally concerned to discredit gradualism.[68]

Actually, there is *no scientific evidence* for either gradual evolution or rapid evolution. All the real facts of science conform precisely to the predictions of special creationism, exactly as taught in the Bible. Christians dare not settle for anything less than this, especially in their own Christian schools.

Now that Soviet style Communism is disintegrating in the former Soviet republics, many people in Russia, Ukraine, and other regions are turning away from atheism, and some even from evolutionism. Unfortunately, however, they are turning in even larger numbers to pantheistic evolutionism or the so-called "New Age" religions. This permits them to believe in a form of religion — specifically pantheism — while still holding fast to evolutionism. Furthermore, the New Age philosophers are also promoting a coming world revolution, and are supporting punctuationism as its scientific justification and pattern. In a sense, therefore, New-Age-ism is a modern offshoot of Marxism,[69] and this will be discussed in more detail shortly.

In the meantime, modern Darwinian evolutionists, unwilling to give up their faith in slow-and-gradual evolution, are attributing the decline and fall of Soviet Communism to the former long-term promotion of Lamarckian evolution by Russia and her satellites.

> I propose that Stalin's unyielding support of Lamarckian evolutionary theory, which he deemed consistent with Marxist socioeconomic theory, was the final cause of Soviet Communism's collapse.[70]

Although there is still a strong rearguard defense of traditional neo-Darwinism in the traditionally capitalistic countries, it also is under

---

[68] L. B. Halstead, "Museum of Errors," *Nature* (November 20, 1980), p. 280.

[69] Richard Wurmbrand, a pastor long imprisoned in Siberia because of his Christian testimony, argues cogently that Marx was actually a Satanist. See Wurmbrand's book *Marx and Satan* (Westchester, IL: Crossway Books, 1990).

[70] David R. Hickey, "Evolution, Environment, and the Collapse of Soviet Communism," *The Humanist* (January/February 1992), p. 34.

attack by younger evolutionists, as the cause of environmental exploitation and assorted other ills (racism, imperialism, etc.). With both Lamarckianism and Darwinism on the wane, many creationists are celebrating too soon, citing with relish the writings of such anti-Darwinists as Lovtrup, Hoyle, Denton, and others, apparently not realizing that New Age pantheistic evolutionism, which in effect they are promoting (being unwilling to accept true monotheistic creationism, as revealed in Genesis), is destined prophetically to be the religion of the coming world government of Antichrist.

Evolution and the New Age

A strange religion has been coming into prominence in recent years. Sometimes mis-called the "New Age Movement," this phenomenon is in reality a complex of modern science and ancient paganism, featuring systems theory, computer science, and mathematical physics, along with astrology, occultism, religious mysticism, and nature worship. Ostensibly offered as a reaction against the sterile materialism of Western thought, this influential system appeals both to man's religious nature and to his intellectual pride. Its goal is to become the world's one religion.

Although New Agers have a form of religion, their "god" is evolution, not the true God of creation. Many of them regard the controversial priest, Teilhard de Chardin, as their spiritual father. His famous statement of faith is as follows:

> [Evolution] is a general postulate to which all theories, all hypotheses, all systems must henceforward bow and which they must satisfy in order to be thinkable and true. Evolution is a light which illuminates all facts, a trajectory which all lines of thought must follow.[71]

The ethnic religions of the East (Hinduism, Taoism, Buddhism, Confucianism, etc.), which in large measure continue the polytheistic pantheism of the ancient pagan religions, have long espoused evolutionary views of the universe and its living things, and so they merge naturally and easily into the evolutionary framework of the New Age philosophy. It is surprising, however, to find that Julian Huxley and Theodosius Dobzhansky, the two most prominent of the western scientific neo-Darwinians, were really early proponents of this modern evolutionary religion. In a eulogy following Dobzhansky's death,

---

[71] Cited in "Nothing in Biology Makes Sense Except in the Light of Evolution: Theodosius Dobzhansky, 1900-1975," by Francisco Ayala, in *Journal of Heredity*, vol. 68, no. 3 (1977), p. 3.

geneticist Francisco Ayala said:

> Dobzhansky was a religious man, although he apparently rejected fundamental beliefs of traditional religion, such as the existence of a personal God. . . . Dobzhansky held that in man, biological evolution has transcended itself into the realm of self-awareness and culture. He believed that mankind would eventually evolve into higher levels of harmony and creativity. He was a metaphysical optimist.[72]

Dobzhansky himself penned the following typical New Age sentiment:

> In giving rise to man, the evolutionary process has, apparently for the first and only time in the history of the Cosmos, become conscious of itself.[73]

Sir Julian Huxley, probably the foremost evolutionist of the 20th century, and the first Director-General of UNESCO, had great plans for what he wanted to make the world's one religion.

> The beliefs of this religion of evolutionary humanism are not based on revelation in the supernatural sense, but on the revelations that science and learning have given us about man and the universe. A humanist believes with full assurance that man is not alien to nature, but a part of nature, albeit a unique one. . . . His future destiny is to guide the future course of evolution on earth towards greater fulfillment, . . . the Fulfillment Society.[74]

More recently, the socialist Jeremy Rifkin expressed this concept in picturesque language, as follows:

> Evolution is no longer viewed as a mindless affair, quite the opposite. It is mind enlarging its domain up the chain of species.[75]

In this way one eventually ends up with the idea of the

---

[72] Cited in "Nothing in Biology Makes Sense Except in the Light of Evolution: Theodosius Dobzhansky, 1900-1975," by Francisco Ayala, in *Journal of Heredity*, vol. 68, no. 3 (1977), p. 9.

[73] Theodosius Dobzhansky, "Changing Man," *Science*, vol. 155 (January 27, 1967), p. 409.

[74] Julian Huxley, "The Coming New Religion of Humanism," *The Humanist* (January/February 1962).

[75] Jeremy Rifkin, *Algeny* (New York, NY: Viking Press, 1983), p. 188.

> universe as a mind that oversees, orchestrates, and gives order and structure to all things.[76]

Lest anyone misunderstand, this universal mind is not intended to represent the God of the Bible at all. Harvard University's Nobel prize-winning biologist George Wald, who used to state that he didn't even like to use the word "God" in a sentence, has come to realize that the complex organization of the universe cannot be due to chance, and so has become an advocate of this modernized form of pantheism. He maintains:

> There are two major problems rooted in science, but unassimilable as science, consciousness and cosmology. . . . The universe wants to be known. Did the universe come about to play its role to empty benches?[77]

Modern physicists have played a key role in the recent popularization of evolutionary pantheism, with what they have called the "anthropic principle."

> At least the anthropic principle suggests connections between the existence of man and aspects of physics that one might have thought would have little bearing on biology. In its strongest form the principle might reveal that the universe we live in is the only conceivable universe in which intelligent life could exist.[78]

This remarkable compatibility of the universe with its human occupants is not accepted as a testimony to divine design, however, but as a deterministic outcome of the "cosmic mind." The anthropic principle is emphasized in a quasi-official "New Age" publication as follows:

> Given the facts, our existence seems quite improbable — more miraculous, perhaps, than the seven-day wonder of Genesis. As physicist Freeman Dyson of the Institute for Advanced Study in Princeton, New Jersey, once remarked, "The universe in some sense must have known we were coming."[79]

---

[76] *Ibid.*, p. 195.

[77] George Wald, as reported in "A Knowing Universe Seeking to be Known," by Dietrick E. Thomsen, *Science News*, vol. 123 (February 19, 1983), p. 124.

[78] George Gale, "The Anthropic Principle," *Scientific American*, vol. 245 (December 1981), p. 154.

[79] Judith Hooper, "Perfect Timing," *New Age Journal*, vol. 11 (December 1985), p. 18.

Prior to these modern developments, Sir Julian Huxley, arguably the leading architect of the neo-Darwinian system, had written an influential book called *Religion without Revelation*, and had become, with John Dewey, a chief founder of the American Humanist Association. As first Director-General of UNESCO, he formulated the principles of what he hoped would soon become the official religion of the world:

> Thus, the general philosophy of UNESCO should, it seems, be a scientific world humanism, global in extent and evolutionary in background.[80]
>
> The unifying of traditions into a single common pool of experience, awareness and purpose is the necessary prerequisite for further major progress in human evolution. Accordingly, although political unification in some sort of world government will be required for the definitive attainment of this state, unification in the things of the mind is not only necessary also, but it can pave the way for other types of unification.[81]

The neo-Darwinian religionists (Huxley, Dobzhansky, Dewey, etc.) thought that evolutionary gradualism would become the basis for the coming world humanistic religion. Evolutionists of the new generation, on the other hand, have increasingly turned to punctuationism — or revolutionary evolutionism — as the favored rationale, largely because of the scientific fallacies in gradualism increasingly exposed by creationists. This development has facilitated the amalgamation of Western scientism with Eastern mysticism.

> The new systems biology shows that fluctuations are crucial in the dynamics of self-organization. They are the basis of order in the living world: ordered structures arise from rhythmic patterns. . . . The idea of fluctuations as the basis of order . . . is one of the major themes in all Taoist texts. The mutual interdependence of all aspects of reality and the nonlinear nature of its interconnections are emphasized throughout Eastern mysticism.[82]

---

[80] Julian Huxley, "A New World Vision," *The Humanist*, vol. 39, (March/April 1979), p. 35.

[81] *Ibid.* This paper was kept "in-house" by UNESCO for about 30 years, before *The Humanist* was allowed to publish it.

[82] Fritjof Capra, "The Dance of Life," *Science Digest*, vol. 90 (April 1982), p. 33.

The author quoted here, Dr. Fritjof Capra, at the University of California (Berkeley), is one of the New Age movement's main scientific theoreticians, particularly in the application of modern computerized networking and systems analysis to the study of past and future evolution, also appropriating the unscientific idea of "order through chaos," an ancient pagan notion reintroduced to modern thought by Ilya Prigogine.

The incorporation of Eastern religious evolutionism into Western evolutionary thought was greatly facilitated also by the "Aquarian Age" emphasis of the student revolution of the sixties. Not all of the scientific "New Agers" accept the astrological and occult aspects of the movement, but even these features are becoming more prominent and intellectually acceptable with the growth of its pantheistic dimensions. John Allegro makes the following ominous prediction:

> It may be that, despite our rightly prized rationality, religion still offers man his best chance of survival. . . . If so, it must be a faith that offers something more than a formal assent to highly speculative dogma about the nature of a god and his divine purpose in creation; it must promise its adherents a living relationship that answers man's individual needs within a formal structure of communal worship. . . . Historically, the cult of the Earth Mother, the ancient religion of the witches, has probably come nearest to fulfilling this role, and being sexually oriented has been especially concerned with this most disturbing and potentially disruptive element in man's biological constitution.[83]

A brilliant modern scientist with a Ph.D. in cell biology from Cambridge, with further studies at Harvard, has discussed the Gaia concept (*Gaia* was the supposed Greek goddess of the earth, essentially equivalent to Mother Earth) as follows:

> Thus through Darwin's theory, nature took on the creative powers of the Great Mother, powers quite unsuspected in the original mechanistic conception of nature. Evolutionary philosophers conceived of these powers in a variety of ways. In the dialectical materialism of Marx and Engels, the creative mother principle is matter, undergo-

---

[83] John M. Allegro, "Divine Discontent," *American Atheist*, vol. 28 (September 1986), p. 30.

ing a continual spontaneous process of development, resolving conflicts and contradictions in successive syntheses. In the philosophy of Herbert Spencer, progressive evolution itself was the supreme principle of the entire universe. The vitalist philosopher Henri Bergson attributed the creativity of evolution to a vital impetus, the elan vital. In his view, the evolutionary process is not designed and planned in advance in the mind of a transcendent God, but is spontaneous and creative.[84]

"Gaia," the religion of the Earth Mother — Mother Nature — is essentially ancient pantheism. It is now returning, even in "Christian lands," in all its demonic power! When combined with the pervasive controls made possible by modern computerized systems technology, the global goals of evolutionary humanism seem very imminent indeed. Jeremy Rifkin considers them to be inevitable.

> We no longer feel ourselves to be guests in someone else's home and therefore obliged to make our behavior conform with a set of pre-existing cosmic rules. It is our creation now. We make the rules. We establish the parameters of reality. We create the world, and because we do, we no longer feel beholden to outside forces. We no longer have to justify our behavior, for we are now the architects of the universe. We are responsible to nothing outside ourselves, for we are the kingdom, the power, and the glory forever and ever.[85]

Rifkin, though certain this is the world's future, is, nevertheless, despondent. He closes his book with these words of despair:

> Our future is secured. The cosmos wails.[86]

New Age evolutionism is not so new, after all, and Mother Nature is really nothing but one of the many faces of ancient Babylon, the "Mother of Harlots" (Rev. 17:5), the age-old religion of God's ancient enemy, Satan, "which deceiveth the whole world" (Rev. 12:9).

Scientifically speaking, New Age evolutionism, with its absurd ideas of order through chaos and quantum speciations, is even less

---

[84] Rupert Sheldrake, *The Rebirth of Nature: The Greening of Science and of God* (New York, NY: Bantam Books, 1991), p. 71.

[85] Jeremy Rifkin, *Algeny*, p. 244.

[86] *Ibid.*, p. 255.

defensible than Darwinian gradualism. Biblically speaking, evolutionism in any form is false. "For in six days the Lord made heaven and earth, the sea, and all that in them is" (Exod. 20:11). Instead of a wailing cosmos, "the heavens declare the glory of God, and the firmament sheweth His handiwork" (Ps. 19:1). The real "new age" will come when Christ returns!

Few people today seem to realize that evolutionism has been around ever since Satan's fall. In ancient religious systems, it was commonly incorporated with pantheism, the belief that nature itself, or the cosmos, is "god." The cosmos (space and time and primeval matter) is the "creator" of all things; there is no personal transcendent God of creation such as revealed in the Bible.

Ever since Darwin, the concept of natural selection has dominated evolutionary thought, providing a "naturalistic" explanation for the origin of species, and thus (as Julian Huxley used to say) eliminating the need for God. In recent years, the strong reaction against Darwinian evolution in many places has caused these scientists to turn to pre-Darwinian evolutionism. That is, they are abandoning atheistic evolution and returning to pantheistic evolution, the pseudo-scientific rationale underlying the New Age movement.

Dr. Stanley Jaki, with doctorates in both physics and theology and author of 32 books, confirms the universality of ancient pagan evolutionism:

> All of these ancients were pagan. The essence of paganism, old and new, is that the universe is eternal, that its motions are without beginning and without end. Belief in creation out of nothing is the very opposite of paganism.[87]

As far as the post-Flood world is concerned, this pagan evolutionism originated in ancient Babylon, in the land of Sumer, but then spread around the world with the dispersion, as described in Genesis 11. It came to full flower in Greece, especially through the writings of Homer and Hesiod.

The earth itself was known as the mother of all living things. The Greek goddess of the earth, Gaia (with equivalent names in other ethnic religions), soon became recognized as "Mother Earth" or "Mother Nature."

---

[87] Stanley L. Jaki, "Science: Western or What?" *Intercollegiate Review*, vol. 26 (Fall 1990), p. 8.

> How did we reach our present secular humanist world? In times that are ancient by human measure, as far back as the earliest artifacts can be found, it seems that the Earth was worshipped as a goddess and believed to be alive. The myth of the great Mother is part of most early religions.[88]

The author cited above is a brilliant scientist and is one of the leaders in developing the modern "Gaian Hypothesis," which views the earth as an actual living organism, evolving itself while controlling the geological evolution of its crust and the biological evolution of its plants and animals.

> The evolution of the species and the evolution of their environment are tightly coupled together as a single and inseparable process.[89]

Lovelock and other leading Gaians do not think of Gaia as a real woman living on Mount Olympus or somewhere, but as a living, intelligent "being," comprising the earth and all its evolving organisms and other systems. Neither Lovelock nor his followers think of Gaia as an actual personal "goddess," or anything of the sort:

> In no way do I see Gaia as a sentient being, a surrogate God. To me Gaia is alive and part of the ineffable Universe and I am a part of her.[90]

Another distinguished scientist advocating evolutionary pantheism is Rupert Sheldrake with a Ph.D. from Cambridge University, and later director of studies in cell biology there.

> But today, with the rise of the green movement, Mother Nature is reasserting herself, whether we like it or not. In particular, the acknowledgment that our planet is a living organism, Gaia, Mother Earth, strikes a responsive chord in millions of people.[91]

As Dr. Sheldrake indicates, the modern "green movement," which is rapidly growing all over the world, is largely committed to this

---

[88] James Lovelock, *The Ages of Gaia* (New York, NY: W. W. Norton and Co., 1988), p. 208.
[89] *Ibid.*, p. 12.
[90] *Ibid.*, p. 218.
[91] Sheldrake, *The Rebirth of Nature*, p. 10.

concept of pantheistic evolution. In fact, the environmental activists in politics, both local and national, are also strongly influenced by such ideas.

> Lovelock's musings have had two consequences. They inspired a quasi-political movement based in London, complete with a publishing arm, that now includes thousands of adherents throughout the U.S. and Western Europe: it appeals naturally to scientifically innocent individuals who worry about the environment.[92]

Sheldrake is careful to point out also that this New-Age evolutionary pantheism is essentially a revival of the ancient religions.

> Although there was much debate over the details, animism was central to Greek thinking. The great philosophers believed that the world of nature was alive because of its ceaseless motion. Moreover, because these motions were regular and orderly, they said that the world of nature was not only alive but intelligent, a vast animal with a soul and a rational mind of its own.[93]

The effect of evolutionism on the environmental movement and related topics will be discussed in the next chapter. In the meantime, it has become compellingly evident that the tree of evolution has borne an abundance of corrupt fruit, in both theory and practice, and Christians should never partake of it.

This pantheistic theme is being continually emphasized in public school classrooms today. The nation even elected in 1992 a vice president whose best-selling book, *Earth in the Balance: Ecology and the Human Spirit,* was passionately devoted to such concepts.[94]

The worship of "Mother Earth" is also becoming prominent in some aspects of the modern feminist movement. The more radical feminists, in fact, are replacing God with "the Goddess," even holding worship services in "her" name. In fact, Vice President Al Gore, on page 260 of his book, cites with approval the statement that "the prevailing ideology of belief in prehistoric Europe and much of the world was based on the worship of a single earth goddess," lamenting the fact that "organized goddess worship was eliminated by Christianity."[95]

---

[92] Tim Beardsley, "Gaia," *Scientific American*, vol. 261 (December 1989), p. 35.

[93] Sheldrake, *The Rebirth of Nature*, p. 44.

[94] Al Gore, *Earth in the Balance: Ecology and the Human Spirit* (1992).

[95] *Ibid.*, p. 260.

In fact, the idea of pantheistic evolution is not even limited to that of Earth and its systems. Modern New Agers embrace the whole universe in some form of conscious cosmic evolution. The famous astronomer Fred Hoyle, in fact, has written an entire book[96] rejecting terrestrial Darwin-type evolution, in favor of cosmic pantheistic evolution. Another British astronomer and physicist, Paul Davies, thinks that modern notions of "order from chaos" somehow prove that the "creative cosmos" has created itself.

> In recent years, more scientists have come to recognize that matter and energy possess an innate ability to self-organize.[97]

Then, continuing, Davies presumably proves this merely by citing the following:

> The astonishing ability of an embryo to develop from a single strand of DNA, via an exquisitely well-organized sequence of formative steps, into an exceedingly complex organism.[98]

Dr. Davies neglects to explain, however, just *how* the DNA was ever programmed to do this. Perhaps Mother Nature did it! In any case, this is exactly what more and more scientists believe today.

> All nature is evolutionary. The cosmos is like a great developing organism, and evolutionary creativity is inherent in nature herself.[99]

But that is not all.

> The universe as a whole is a developing organism, and so are the galaxies, solar systems, and biospheres within it, including the earth.[100]

It is not necessary to discuss this further here, but the fact is that there is no more scientific proof (or even real evidence) for *pantheistic* evolution than there is for *atheistic* evolution. Evolution in any form is nothing but "cunningly devised fables" and "science falsely so-called."[101]

---

[96] Fred Hoyle, *The Intelligent Universe* (London: Michael Joseph Co., 1983).

[97] Paul Davies, "The Creative Cosmos," *New Scientist*, vol. 116 (December 17, 1987), p. 42.

[98] *Ibid.*

[99] Sheldrake, *op. cit.*, p. 95.

[100] *Ibid.*, p. 151.

[101] 2 Peter 1:16; 1 Timothy 6:20.

The Catholic physicist, Dr. Wolfgang Smith, has said:

> The point, however, is that the doctrine of evolution has swept the world, not on the strength of its scientific merits, but precisely in its capacity as a Gnostic myth. It affirms, in effect, that living beings created themselves, which is, in essence, a metaphysical claim. . . . Thus, in the final analysis, evolutionism is in truth a metaphysical doctrine decked out in scientific garb.[102]

Just as pantheistic evolution served as the world's religion in the early days, so it will do again in the last days. The New Age is really nothing but a revival in modern garb of the Old Age — that is, the first age after the Flood, when King Nimrod led the world in a united rebellion against the Creator (Gen. 10:8-12; 11:1-9). And just as all the groups in the wide spectrum of New Age beliefs are founded upon a base of pantheistic evolutionism, so all have as their ultimate goal, just as Nimrod did, the development of a global system of government, culture, finance, and religion. The United Nations Organization is currently the focus of these plans, but it will eventually "evolve" into a much stronger international government, in which all "the kings of the earth [will] set themselves, and the rulers take counsel together, against the Lord, and against His [Christ], saying, Let us break their bands asunder, and cast away their cords from us" (Ps. 2:2, 3).

To accomplish this, the evolutionary pantheists must first teach men once again (as they did in ancient time) to change "the glory of the uncorruptible God into an image made like to corruptible man," and then to "[worship] and [serve] the creature more than the Creator" (Rom. 1:23, 25). Robert Muller, former Assistant Secretary General of the United Nations (presumably speaking on behalf of that organization) has expressed their hope thus:

> I believe the most fundamental thing we can do today is to believe in evolution.[103]

Now, if the most fundamental thing that New Agers (as well as the older-style secular humanists and social Darwinists) can do to bring about such a world system is to believe in evolution, that means the most

---

[102] Wolfgang Smith, *Teilhardism and the New Religion* (Rockford, IL: Tan Books and Publishers, 1988), p. 242.

[103] Robert Muller, as cited in "United Nations' Robert Muller — a Vistion of Global Spirituality," by Kristin Murphy, *The Movement Newspaper* (September 1983), p. 10.

effective thing the remnant of believers in God and His Word can do to offset this is to believe and teach a soundly biblical and scientific creationism. This must include the great truth that the Creator has now also become the Lamb of God, our sin-forgiving Saviour, and soon will return as eternal King.

In that day, "These shall make war with the Lamb, and the Lamb shall overcome them: for He is Lord of lords, and King of kings" (Rev. 17:14).

Chapter 5

Evolution Everywhere

We have now seen the pervasiveness of evolutionary philosophy in every field of study, as well as its long, long history as the basic weapon in Satan's warfare against his Creator. We have also noted that evolutionism has been used as the pseudo-scientific justification for almost every deadly philosophy and every evil practice known to man. In this chapter, the impact of the creation/evolution issue on a variety of current social problems will be reviewed.

Many of these current problems seem to be closely associated with the New Age movement and its revival of ancient pantheistic evolutionism, as just discussed in the preceding chapter. Perhaps the most visible and abrasive of these current problems is what has been variously called the ecological crisis, the environmental movement or the Green Party. As we shall see, however, to the extent that there is an environmental crisis, it has been brought about by evolutionists, not by biblical Christians, as some have alleged.

Creation, Evolution, and Ecology

The essence of evolutionism was expressed by Charles Darwin in the very last paragraph of his *Origin of Species* as follows:

> Thus, from the war of nature, from famine and death, the most exalted object which we are capable of conceiving, the production of the higher animals, directly follows.[1]

The struggle for existence, with elimination of the weak and unfit, leads to survival of the fittest, so this war of nature must eventually lead to higher animals, higher races, and finally to higher civilizations. Or so

[1] Charles Darwin, *Origin of Species*, all editions, final paragraph.

goes the rationale for Social Darwinism, as exploited especially by Darwin's disciples in the century following the publication of his book.

Among other harmful results of this philosophy has been the thoughtless exploitation of our natural resources during the past century — mineral, animal, and human resources — all in the name of socio-economic evolution.

Great mineral and timber resources have been wastefully misused, and many plant and animal species have become extinct, in many cases because of careless human activities. It has been estimated by Myers that at least 1,000 species are becoming extinct every year. Then he adds this warning:

> If current land-use patterns and environment-destruction patterns persist (and many are likely to accelerate), the extinction rate could surely rise by the year 2000 to an average of 100 species per day.[2]

Evolutionists have tried to blame this ecological catastrophe on biblical creationism, even though the real cause was the attitude of Social Darwinism that prevailed during the post-Darwin century. In a widely quoted article, "The Historical Roots of our Ecologic Crisis," historian Lynn White charges, for example, that the Christian concept of a transcendent God has been used to justify this insensitivity to nature. In his last paragraph, White summarizes his argument as follows:

> Both our present science and our present technology are so tinctured with orthodox Christian arrogance toward nature that no solution for our ecologic crisis can be expected from them alone. Since the roots of our trouble are so largely religious, the remedy must also be essentially religious, whether we call it that or not. We must re-think and re-feel our nature and destiny.[3]

The religion that White and most modern environmentalists advocate, is some form of pantheism. Pantheism is also based on evolution, of course, but it is a different kind of evolution than Darwinism. Most New Agers are opposed to Darwinism, because they recognize the folly of its pseudo-science and the cruelty of its motivations. But they are

---

[2] Norman Myers, "Extinction Rates Past and Present," *Bioscience*, vol. 39 (January 1989), p. 39.

[3] Lynn White, "The Historical Roots of our Ecologic Crisis," *Science*, vol. 155 (March 10, 1967), p. 1207.

evolutionists nonetheless, bitterly opposed to the Creator God of the Bible. Instead, they "worship and serve the creature more than the Creator" (Rom. 1:25).

They are wrong, however, in attributing our "ecologic crisis" to the Creator and His "dominion mandate," even though there are, no doubt, some Christians who have indeed been insensitive to nature. In fact, many of the "Social Darwinists" of the 19th and 20th centuries were "theistic" evolutionists, and were so enamored of the idea of "evolutionary progress," that they worked diligently to harmonize the Bible with that post-Darwinian system.

This was impossible, of course, for the Bible is clearly opposed to *any* form of evolutionism — atheistic, theistic, or pantheistic. The Bible certainly does not condone human cruelty to animals or even to plant life, but it also condemns all forms of nature worship.

Christians today are under many pressures to compromise, either with Darwinian evolutionism on the one hand, or pantheistic (New Age) evolutionism on the other. It is more important than ever, therefore, for us to try to understand the full implications of our relation to God's creation, as well as our personal relation to Him as our Creator and Redeemer.

After God had finished creating all other things, He created man and woman and gave them "dominion over the fish of the sea, and over the fowl of the air, and over the cattle, and over all the earth, and over every creeping thing that creepeth upon the earth" (Gen. 1:26). This "dominion mandate" thus makes a clear distinction between mankind and all the rest of creation, for only men and women were created "in the image of God" (Gen. 1:27), and were given control "over all the earth." This dominion, however, was not to be a totalitarian despotism, but a stewardship under God, man being responsible to God for its care, "for the earth is the Lord's , and the fulness thereof" (Ps. 24:1).

And God *does care* for His creation; He is not capricious. He is omniscient and omnipotent and has a divine purpose in everything that He created. Before sin and death came into the world, God placed Adam in the Garden of Eden and told him "to dress it and to keep it" (Gen. 2:15). Then, he and Eve were told later that they were to "be fruitful, and multiply, and replenish [i.e., 'fill'] the earth, and subdue it" (Gen. 1:28). The clear implication was that as the population expanded to fill the earth, man's descendants were to "dress and keep" their own respective parts of the earth, just as Adam was to care for his. The work of subduing the earth would involve learning to understand all its processes and all its creatures, for the benefit of mankind and for the glory of God.

This mandate is still in effect today. It applies to all descendants of Adam and Eve, but is even more important for Christians, because we who have been saved have come to know the Lord not only in His work as the world's Creator, but also in His work as the world's Redeemer.

In exercising his dominion over the earth, man has the right to eat of its fruits and herbs (Gen. 1:29) and also the flesh of animals. "For every creature of God is good, and nothing to be refused, if it be received with thanksgiving" (1 Tim. 4:4). Even God, appearing to Abraham in human form, ate of "a calf, tender and good," along with "butter and milk" (Gen. 18:1, 7-8), and Jesus ate of the Passover lamb with His disciples (Luke 22:7-8).

The skins of animals may also be used to make human clothing. John the Baptist, the greatest man ever born of woman, according to Christ, filled with the Holy Spirit from his mother's womb (Matt. 11:11; Luke 1:15), "was clothed with camel's hair, and with a girdle of a skin about his loins" (Mark 1:6). God himself set the pattern after Adam and Eve had sinned, for unto them "did the Lord God make coats of skins, and clothed them" (Gen. 3:21).

Animals were also used, with God's approval, for transportation (Jesus rode into Jerusalem on an ass's colt, for example), to serve as beasts of burden, and as sacrifices for sin. Trees were felled for construction and for firewood, and designated areas (e.g., the valley of Hinnom) were used for refuse disposal. All such uses of the earth and its creatures are evidently recognized by God as necessary and proper in connection with His purposes for man in this present world.

At the same time, we must never forget that we are stewards of God's created world and that He cares deeply for it. "[He] hath measured the waters in the hollow of His hand, and meted out heaven with the span, and comprehended the dust of the earth in a measure, and weighed the mountains in scales, and the hills in a balance" (Isa. 40:12).

Although His greatest provisions are for men and women, He also provides for animals, and even for the land itself, "to cause it to rain on the earth, where no man is; on the wilderness, wherein there is no man; to satisfy the desolate and waste ground; and to cause the bud of the tender herb to spring forth" (Job 38:26-27). "He sendeth the springs into the valleys, which run among the hills. They give drink to every beast of the field: . . . By them shall the fowls of the heaven have their habitation, which sing among the branches. . . . He causeth the grass to grow for the cattle. . . . So is this great and wide sea, wherein are things creeping innumerable. . . . These wait all upon Thee, that Thou mayest give them their meat in due season. . . . They are filled with good" (Ps. 104: 10-12,

14, 25, 27-28). If God is that careful to provide for His creatures, we as His stewards thereof should also care for them.

The creation also provides wonderful instruction for us. The waters speak of life, the fires of judgment, the trees of strength, the vineyards of spiritual fruit. The ants teach industry and the eagles of mounting up toward God. "But ask now the beasts, and they shall teach thee; and the fowls of the air, and they shall tell thee; Or speak to the earth, and it shall teach thee; and the fishes of the sea shall declare unto thee. Who knoweth not in all these that the hand of the Lord hath wrought this?" (Job 12:7-10).

Furthermore, God does not take death lightly, either human death or animal death. Jesus said, "Are not two sparrows sold for a farthing? and one of them shall not fall on the ground without your Father" (Matt. 10:29).

Nor does God condone mistreatment of animals. "For the Scripture saith, Thou shalt not muzzle the ox that treadeth out the corn" (1 Tim. 5:18). God on one occasion even miraculously allowed an animal to protest verbally to its master about its beatings (Num. 22:28). God did not allow His people to "seethe a kid in his mother's milk" (Exod. 23:19), even though the meat of the animal could be eaten by them. He ordained a weekly rest for animals as well as for people. "The seventh day is the sabbath [i.e., 'rest'] of the Lord thy God: in it thou shalt not do any work, . . . nor thy cattle" (Exod. 20:10). He likewise commanded even a sabbatical year of rest for agricultural lands (Lev. 25:3-4).

God lovingly takes care of His creation, and so should we, as His stewards. But we must not worship it, nor consider "nature" as our "Mother Nature." We have not come by evolutionary descent from the animals (or from hydrogen gas!) as the naturalists assert, nor do we have any evolutionary kinship with the animals, as the pantheists teach.

Therefore, every problem of an ecological and environmental nature must be carefully considered in the light of all these truths. There are many such problems: air pollution, water pollution, deforestation, suburban development, agricultural pesticides, toxic wastes, coal mining, animal experimentation, and on and on. The laissez-faire evolutionist may want freedom to spoil the environment unhindered, and the "green-movement" pantheistic evolutionist may want such uses halted altogether, but the will of God should always be the deciding factor.

His will obviously involves an optimum balance between human needs on the one hand, and maintenance of the pristine ecology on the other. Such an optimum balance is rarely perfectly achieved, but this should be man's goal.

Both those who "destroy the earth" (Rev. 11:18), on the one hand, and also those who "worship and serve the creature" (Rom. 1:25), on the other, are under the condemnation of God. Nature is not our "Mother," and Time is not our "Father." All men are the offspring of God by creation (Acts 17:28-29), and redeemed men are the children of God by regeneration through faith in Christ (Gal. 3:26). May God help all of us who know Christ as Creator and Saviour to honor His creation as well.

It is still true, of course, that one of man's most vexing problems today is the tension between the growing need for energy resources and preserving the natural environment, or — putting it another way — between conservation of a standard of living and conservation of nature.

As with all great issues, the way in which a person views a problem and the course of action that he follows in handling it depend fundamentally upon his basic philosophy of life. The ecological crisis, in particular, points up the evolution-creation conflict in a surprising light.

In the first place, the ecological relationships that exist in nature between groups of organisms and their respective environments, or "ecological niches," would seem to indicate an origin by intelligent forethought and planning, not random struggle between populations. The innumerable and remarkable "adaptations" of this sort are very difficult to "explain" in evolutionist terms. Two of the world's leading biological students of ecology pointed this out early in the modern ecology movement.

> Some biologists claim that an understanding of the evolutionary history of organisms is prerequisite to any comprehension of ecology. We believe that this notion is having the effect of sheltering large areas of population biology from the benefits of rigorous thought. . . . Indeed, since the level of speculation rather than investigation is inevitably high in phylogenetic studies of any kind, a preoccupation with the largely unknown past can be shown to be a positive hindrance to progress.[4]

Therefore, a supposed understanding of evolution is of no value in understanding ecology, and its theories are even harmful to a true understanding of modern ecological relationships. Evolutionary ideas concerning these matters, furthermore, are based on theory, not on fact.

> Indeed, we know nothing whatever of the antecedents

[4] Paul R. Ehrlich and L. C. Birch, "Evolutionary History and Population Biology," *Nature*, vol. 214 (April 22, 1967), p. 349.

> of most species for thousands of years. Perhaps these dismal facts account for some of the strangely unsatisfying "explanations" of the evolutionary ecologists.[5]

Since evolution provides no satisfactory explanation of present ecological relationships, it obviously can provide no guidance for future policies on environmental problems. Creationism, however, provides better solutions as to both past developments and future guidelines.

But evolutionists have for many years been propagating the absurd notion that man's exploitation of the world's resources has been based on the supposed biblical teaching that those resources had been made strictly for this exhaustive purpose. The Bible, however, teaches no such thing. If there is to be any placing of blame for the problem of pollution and related ills, it should be assigned to the philosophy of evolution, where it really belongs! Furthermore, effective remedies for such problems can be found only in the context of a sound creationist philosophy.

The essence of naturalistic evolution, of course, is randomness. The evolutionary process supposedly began with random particles, and has continued by random aggregations of matter and then random mutations of genes. The fossil record, as interpreted by evolutionists, is said by them to indicate eons of purposeless evolutionary meanderings, the senseless struggling and dying of untold billions of animals, extinctions of species, misfits, blind alleys. The present-day environmental-ecologic complex then is nothing more than the current stage in this unending *random* struggle for existence.

In recent years, Stephen Jay Gould (probably America's leading evolutionist at present) has insistently pointed out that there is no pattern of "progress" in evolution, no directing program. Everything, including man himself, is merely an accident.

> Nonetheless, contemporary science has massively substituted notions of indeterminacy, historical contingency, chaos and punctuation for previous convictions about gradual, progressive, predictable determinism.[6]

> Humans arose, rather, as a fortuitous and contingent outcome of thousands of linked events, any one of which could have occurred differently and sent history on an

[5] *Ibid.*, p. 351.

[6] Stephen Jay Gould and Niles Eldredge, "Punctuated Equilibrium Comes of Age," *Nature*, vol. 366 (November 18, 1993), p. 227.

alternate pathway that would not have led to consciousness.[7]

Those populations of organisms that have survived to this point, therefore, must somehow represent the "fittest" — those that have been screened and preserved by accident and the process of natural selection. In spite of its randomness, therefore, evolutionists believe that the net result of evolution has somehow been the development of complex kinds, and finally of man himself.

This development is believed by most evolutionists to have been made possible by a peculiar combination of small populations, changing environments, and accelerated mutational pressures (Gould would add natural catastrophic extinctions), a combination which supposedly enables natural selection to function in its remarkable role as "creator" of new and perhaps better kinds of populations.

It might seem, therefore, that anything that would change the environment today (for example, by altering the chemical components of the atmosphere and hydrosphere through pollution), decrease populations (perhaps by war, famine, or pestilence), or increase mutational pressures (such as by increasing the radioactive component of the biosphere through nuclear testing), would contribute positively to further evolution and, therefore, should be encouraged — at least if the Gould school of thought is correct in its understanding of evolutionary mechanisms. In other words, the very processes which modern ecologists most deplore today, are those which they believe to have been the cause of the upward evolution of the biosphere in the past. The tongue-in-cheek conclusion would seem to be that evolution *requires* pollution!

More directly to the point, however, three generations of evolutionary teaching have had the pragmatic result of inducing in man an almost universal self-centeredness. God, if He exists at all, is pushed so far back in time and so far out in space that men no longer are concerned about responsibility to Him. As far as other people are concerned, doesn't nature itself teach that we must struggle and compete for survival? Self-preservation is nature's first law. Race must compete against race, nation against nation, class against class, young against old, poor against rich, man against man. All this is part of the natural — savage, brutal, bloody — struggle.

Two thousand years of Christian teaching linger on to some extent, in modern social concerns and in the diluted esthetics and ethics of our

---

[7] Stephen Jay Gould, "The Evolution of Life on Earth," *Scientific American*, vol. 271 (October 1994), p. 86.

day, but these are easily forgotten when one's self-interests are at stake. Conservationist groups may inveigh against the ecological destruction wrought by the oil and utilities industries, but they do not personally wish to give up their automobiles or electrical appliances, nor to pay the higher prices required if these commodities are to be produced without damage to the environment.

Furthermore, during the past 150 years especially, the very exploitation of nature — its flora and fauna, its resources, and even its human populations — against which environmentalists are protesting, has itself been carried out in the name of science and of evolutionary philosophy (e.g., Social Darwinism). Thus, the modern ecologic crisis is not a product of biblical theology at all, but, rather, of a century of worldwide evolutionary thinking and practice. It is significant that all these environmental problems developed almost entirely within the period when the scientific and industrial establishments were totally committed to an evolutionary philosophy!

Recognition of the world as God's direct creation, on the other hand, should transform man's outlook on nature and his attitude toward other men. The creation is God's unique handiwork and displays His character and glory (Ps. 19:1; Ps. 148; Rev. 5:13). The design and implementation of this marvelous universe and its varied inhabitants were to God a source of great delight (Gen. 1:31; Job 38:4-7; Rev. 4:11). Man was created, not to exploit God's world, but to be His steward, exercising dominion over or maintaining it (Gen. 1:26-28) and "keeping" it (Gen. 2:15).

The primeval world as it came from God's hand was beautiful beyond imagination and perfect in every way as man's home. There was ample food for both man and animals (Gen. 1:29, 30), and each kind had its own ecological niche. Even when God stopped creating (Gen. 2:1-3), He provided abundantly for the maintenance of the creation (Neh. 9:6; Heb. 1:3).

With man's fall and God's curse on his dominion, this pristine perfection radically changed (Gen. 3:17; Rom. 8:20, 22). Every process, henceforth, operated inefficiently, and every system tended toward disintegration. Although the earth's resources remained constant in quantity, their quality could thereafter be maintained only with great difficulty, and only at the cost of drawing excess energy from some other source, and usually requiring extensive human effort!

Not only was the quantity of matter and energy originally intended to be "conserved" (as expressed formally now in our scientific Law of Conservation of Energy), but presumably also the "quality" of energy was not intended to diminish. Not only was energy conserved, but entropy as well; the universe was not designed to "perish," "wax old," and "be changed" (Ps. 102:26), but to be "stablished for ever and ever" (Ps. 148:6). In some unknown manner, no longer operating, the sun's energy probably would have been replenished cyclically, from that radiated into space after some had been used to maintain terrestrial processes.

On the earth itself, none of its resources were intended ever to be depleted, and all processes were to function at perfect efficiency. A great abundance of plant and animal life was soon produced, in response to God's commands (Gen. 1:11, 20, 24), and continued to multiply, storing energy from the sun in an enlarging biosphere. All necessary disintegrative processes (e.g., digestion, etc.) were presumably in balance with the increasing numbers of highly structured organisms. Order and entropy were thus everywhere in balance, as well as matter and energy. Everything was "very good" (Gen. 1:31)!

The Bible gives little information as to such specific energy sources before the Flood, except for the sun itself. At the time of the Deluge, however, the earth's energy balance changed drastically. Its greenhouse-like environment, which had been maintained by "waters above the firmament" (Gen. 1:7), was destroyed when the great canopy of vapor condensed and deluged the entire globe. The tremendous stores of chemical energy in the biosphere of the antediluvian world were partially converted in the resulting cataclysm into great stores of coal, oil, and gas, the so-called "fossil fuels." Much of the incoming solar energy thenceforth would be needed to drive the atmospheric circulations, and to maintain the post-diluvian hydrologic cycle for the earth.

It is significant to realize that today's pollution problems are derived mostly from using energy stores that were produced in the Noachian Deluge! Coal is the fossil product of the terrestrial plant life, and oil probably of the marine animal life, of the rich biosphere that had been created and developed by the Creator in the beginning. These organisms were not originally designed to serve as fuels for man's machines, and it is not surprising that the efficiency of heat engines using them is low, and the waste products are high. Furthermore, they are exhaustible, and the eventual end of economical oil and gas production is a matter of great concern.

In a sense, of course, the burning of these fossil fuels is merely hastening the process of "returning to the dust," which is the present fate of all organic life, under the curse. The waste products, both of the processes of life and of the phenomena of death, have always posed a pollution problem to the environment, but the normal cycles of nature are able to accommodate them in part, and even utilize them (e.g., in the enrichment of the soil, etc.) as long as they are sufficiently dispersed in time and space. When concentrated by abnormal numbers of either men or animals, either in living communities or in massive extinctions, however, such wastes cannot be assimilated, and they initiate various abnormal reactions that accelerate and accentuate environmental decay.

These deleterious changes can be corrected to some extent, but only at the cost of excess energy from other sources and therefore only at great labor and expense. Nuclear energy is one possibility but this, of course, creates its own pollutional problems. Geothermal energy may be a partial answer, in the few regions where it is available. Hydroelectric energy has already been developed to nearly its maximum potential in many parts of the world, and is seriously limited in all parts of the world. The energy in the tides and ocean waves is considerable, but its harnessing is economically feasible in only very restricted localities.

Solar energy is undoubtedly the best ultimate hope for an adequate energy supply, since the sun is the ultimate source of energy for all of earth's processes anyhow. To date, however, no economically efficient solar converters have been developed, except for special and limited applications. Since the sun was created to "give light upon the earth" (Gen. 1:17), and since "there is nothing hid from the heat thereof" (Ps. 19:6), we may well believe that it is possible to find ways to utilize solar energy to meet all of man's legitimate energy needs and to do so with a minimal amount of further damage to the environment. Cost of the needed research should not be prohibitive, at least in relation to other energy and environmental costs.

In any case, a creationist orientation can certainly contribute more effectively to the alleviation of such problems, than can an evolutionary perspective. The creationist recognizes that the world is God's handiwork and that he is God's steward. The divine commission to "have dominion over" and to "subdue" the earth is not a license for despotic exploitation of its resources, but rather a call to service, encouraging man to understand its nature ("science") and then to utilize its resources ("technology") for the benefit of all men, under God.

Eventually, however, if the present world (no matter how carefully its resources were guarded) were to continue indefinitely operating under the present laws of nature, it would die. The "whole creation" is under the "bondage of decay" (Rom. 8:20-22).

But this bleak prospect will never be reached. God's eternal purpose in creation cannot fail. The creation, therefore, must be somehow redeemed and saved. Although in the present order, the curse is universal and inexorable, the One who imposed it can also remove it (Rev. 22:3).

The redemption price has, in fact, been paid in full (Col. 1:20), and this "redemption of the purchased possession" (Eph. 1:14) will be completely implemented when Christ returns. At that time, everything, including the earth and its land-water-air environment, will all be "[made] new" again (Rev. 21:5), and will then last forever!

In the meantime, every person who has appropriated this redemption individually through an act of faith in his Creator and Redeemer has the privilege of sharing in God's work of reconciliation, for "He hath given to us the ministry of reconciliation" (2 Cor. 5:18). The work of redemption and reconciliation involves the reclamation and saving both of individual persons and of man's dominion, for the eternal ages to come. We seek not only to win scientists to Christ, but even to win the sciences themselves to Christ.

"O Lord, how manifold are thy works! in wisdom hast thou made them all: the earth is full of thy riches. . . . The glory of the Lord shall endure for ever: the Lord shall rejoice in His works" (Ps. 104:24, 31).

Evolution and the Population Problem

One of the more disturbing aspects of the environmental movement is the propaganda associated with the so-called "population bomb." Because of the environmentalists' fear that the earth's population is about to exceed the planet's resources, all sorts of dangerous measures are being proposed and, in some cases, enforced by government. The number of children in Chinese families, for example, is severely restricted. Abortion and homosexuality, once absolutely illegal in most countries, are now not only legal, but positively encouraged in this country and many others, not only as civil rights but also as positive means of population control. Euthanasia and even infanticide are beginning to be promoted in various places with similar justification. Birth control devices are being discussed and freely distributed in many public schools. The feminist movement is, in many respects, denigrating the role of wife and mother. All of these measures have surely slowed or halted the growth of populations in many of the more developed countries, though the growth rate continues high in many Third World nations.

The "carrying capacity" of planet Earth is finite, of course, but the fact is that it is far from being reached as yet. And the interesting thing about all this is that, if evolution were really true, the earth would have been literally overrun with people long ago!

The intellectual and educational establishments today assume it as self-evident that population growth should be halted. Famed anthropologist Margaret Mead said, more than two decades ago:

> The United Nations Population Conference, which concluded on 31 August in Bucharest, passed by acclamation a World Plan of Action that dramatized the growing global concern for the planet's plight. . . . At Bucharest it was affirmed that continuing, unrestricted worldwide population growth can negate any socio-economic gains and fatally imperil the environment. . . . Those governments for which excessive population growth is detrimental to their national purpose are given a target date of 1985 to provide information and methods for implementing these goals.[8]

The cause for such concern is the supposed excessive rate of world population increase and the fear that this presages the imminent depletion of the world's capacity to sustain its inhabitants. Two of the leading specialists in this field, Donald Freedman, professor of sociology at the University of Michigan, and Bernard Berelson, president of the Population Council, defined the problem as follows:

> In the 1970s the rate of increase has slightly exceeded 2 percent per year. That means a doubling time of less than 35 years, and the number currently being doubled is a very large one. Projection of such growth for very long into the future produces a world population larger than the most optimistic estimates of the planet's carrying capacity.[9]

So urgent did the experts consider this problem to be that the United Nations Organization actually proclaimed 1974 to be "World Population Year." It can be shown, in fact, that if the population continued to increase at the rate of 2 percent per year, in fewer than 700 years there would be one person for every square foot of the earth's surface. Obviously, the present growth rate cannot continue indefinitely.

Nevertheless, creationists find such arguments unconvincing. Since the evidence for a purposeful Creator of the world and mankind is exceedingly strong, the creationist is confident that the world God made for man is large enough and productive enough to accomplish His

---

[8] Margaret Mead, "World Population: World Responsibility," *Science*, vol. 185 (September 27, 1974), p. 1113.

[9] Donald Freedman and Bernard Berelson, "The Human Population," *Scientific American*, vol. 231 (September 1974), p. 31.

purpose. That purpose will surely have been consummated before the population exceeds its divinely intended maximum.

According to the biblical record of creation, immediately after the first man and woman were created, God instructed them as follows:

> Be fruitful, and multiply, and replenish [literally, "fill"] the earth, and subdue it (Gen. 1:28).

Essentially the same commandment was given to the handful of survivors of the great Flood (Gen. 9:1). Since man has not yet come anywhere near to *filling* the earth (the total population currently averages less than one person for every 300,000 square feet of land area), it seems unlikely that the earth has yet reached its optimal population, as far as the purposes of the Creator are concerned. The divine command, no doubt, at least envisioned colonizing all parts of the earth and occupying each part to its potential maximum productive capacity.

Throughout the Scriptures, a large family is considered to be a blessing from the Lord (note Ps. 127:3-5; 128:1-6, etc.), not a problem to society, assuming, of course, that these children are going to be brought up "in the nurture and admonition of the Lord" (Eph. 6:4).

The historic fact of creation is prophetic of the future fact of consummation. Many current trends seem to have been predicted in the Bible and, therefore, suggest that the return of Christ and the end of the age may be near at hand. It is, therefore, at least a possibility that the Creator's work of consummation may solve the population "problem" long before it becomes critical.

Even apart from biblical revelation, however, there is no good reason for alarm over population. The earth is quite able to support a much larger population than it now possesses. Even with the present status of technology (available water for irrigation, potentially arable land, modern methods of soil treatment, and improved crop yields, etc.), authorities estimate that the earth's reasonable "carrying capacity" is about 50 billion people.[10] Future advances in technology (solar energy, saline conversion, etc.), may well increase this still more.

Therefore, even at the present annual increase of 1.6 percent, it will still be well over 100 years before this maximum population will be reached. However, in order for such a population to be achieved, modern technological knowledge will have to be employed worldwide, in the underdeveloped countries as well as in the developed nations. In turn, experience in the latter shows that population growth rates tend to drop

---

[10] Roger Revelle, "Food and Population," *Scientific American*, vol. 231 (September 1974), p. 168. Revelle was director of the Center for Population Studies at Harvard.

off as a society's technology increases. Revelle commented on this as follows:

> Here we are faced with a paradox: attainment of the earth's maximum carrying capacity for human beings would require a high level of agricultural technology, which in turn calls for a high level of social and economic development. Such developments, however, would be likely to lead to a cessation of population growth long before the maximum carrying capacity is reached.[11]

It is interesting that, for the most part, those intellectuals who have been most vocal in support of population limitation (Margaret Mead, for example), are also strong believers in human evolution. This is probably because of their refusal to recognize divine purpose in the world. If there were no creation and, therefore, no purpose or goal in creation, as leading evolutionists believe, then neither is there any reason to believe that the Creator will accomplish His purpose at the end of history. Just as man's past evolution, then, was dependent solely on random natural processes, so must his future be controlled by naturalism, the only difference being that man now knows how to control those processes — or so he hopes.

One of the strange aberrations of the modern drive for ecological and population controls is the notion that the "environmental crisis" is an outgrowth of the biblical teaching that man should multiply numerically and subdue the earth. Professor Lynn White of U.C.L.A. first popularized the perverse notion that this Genesis mandate has served as man's justification for the exploitation of the earth's resources.[12] Professor Richard Means and others have even proposed that we should all revert to belief in a pantheistic polytheism in order to have a proper regard for all aspects of the world and its living things as they have evolved.[13]

This idea is a notable example of evolutionistic confusion of thinking. Christian scholars have never advanced Genesis 1:28 in support of the careless use and waste of any of the earth's resources. To the contrary, since everything is presented in Scripture as the product of God's creative design and purpose, biblical creationist Christians regard themselves and man in general as stewards of the whole creation, accountable to the Creator for its proper development and use.

On the other hand, it is very significant that all of the earth's serious

---

[11] *Ibid.*, p. 169.

[12] Lynn White, "Historical Roots of Ecologic Crisis," p. 1203-1207.

[13] Richard L. Means, "Why Worry about Nature," *Saturday Review* (December 2, 1967).

environmental problems, even its population crisis, have developed during that one century when the evolutionary philosophy had effectively replaced creationism in the thinking of the world's leaders in education, science, and industry. The earth has been exploited not because of any biblical divine mandate, but because of Social Darwinism, economic and military imperialism, secular materialism, anarchistic individualism, and other such applications of the "struggle and survival" rationale of modern evolutionism!

As far as reverting to pantheism is concerned, this is simply another variant of evolutionism, and it will inevitably lead to similar results. The most pantheistic of nations (e.g., India with its Hinduism, China with its Buddhism and Confucianism, etc.) are precisely those nations in which the population/resource ratios have been most severe. It has not been the Judaeo-Christian nations in which population has become a problem, but those with religions of pantheism. How, then, can pantheism solve the very problems it nurtures?

But there is an even greater inconsistency in evolutionary thinking relative to population. The same population statistics that supposedly presage a serious population problem in the future also indicate a very recent origin of man in the past.

To illustrate the problem, assume that the human population increases geometrically (as believed by Thomas Malthus, whose writings were of profound influence on the theories of Charles Darwin). That is, the increase each year is equal to a constant proportion of the population the previous year. This relationship can be expressed algebraically as follows:

Equation (1): $$P_n = P\,(1 + r)^n$$

in which P is the population at any certain time, r is the proportionate annual increase in population, and P_n is the population n years later. For example, if the present population is 5 billion and the planet's permissible population is 50 billion, the number of years before this number of persons will be reached at the present 2 percent annual increase can be calculated as follows:

$$50 \times 10^9 = 5 \times 10^9(1.02)^n$$

from which $$\log \frac{50}{5} = n \log 1.02$$

and $$n = \frac{1}{0.0086} = 116 \text{ years}$$

We have already discussed this result, however. Looking toward the past, instead of the future, equation (1) will also indicate how long it would take to produce the present population at 2 percent growth per year, starting with two people, and calculating as follows:

$$5 \times 10^9 = 2(1.02)^n$$

from which $$n = \frac{9+\log\left(\frac{5}{2}\right)}{\log 1.02} = 1{,}093 \text{ years}$$

That is, an initial population of only two people, increasing at 2 percent per year, would become 5 billion people in only 1,093 years. Since written records go back more than 4,000 years, it is obvious that the average growth rate throughout past history has been considerably less than the present rate.

As a matter of interest, we can also use equation (1) to determine what the average growth rate would have to be to generate the present population in 4,000 years, as follows:

$$5 \times 10^9 = 2(l + r)^{4000}$$

from which $$r = (2.5 \times 10^9)^{\frac{1}{4000}} - 1 = \frac{1}{2}\ \%$$

Thus, an average population growth rate of only 1/2 percent would generate the present world population in only 4000 years. This is only one-fourth of the present rate of growth.

Now, although it is obvious that the present rate of growth (2 percent) could not have prevailed for very long in the past, it does seem very unlikely that the growth rate could have averaged significantly less than 1/2 percent. Very little is known about the world population in earlier times, but everything that is known indicates that the population has steadily increased throughout recorded history.

Dr. Ansley J. Coale, director of the Office of Population Research at Princeton University, has discussed the paucity of such data in an important study.

> Any numerical description of the development of the human population cannot avoid conjecture, simply because there has never been a census of all the people of the world. . . . The earliest date for which the global population can be calculated with an uncertainty of only, say 20 per cent, is the middle of the 18th century. The next earlier time

for which useful data are available is the beginning of the Christian era, when Rome collected information bearing on the number of people in various parts of the empire.[14]

The usually accepted estimates of world population for these two dates are, respectively, about 200 million in A.D. 1, and about one billion in A.D. 1800. The first, however, may be vastly in error, since no one really knows the population in most parts of the world at that early date.

For earlier periods than A.D. 1, absolutely nothing is known concerning world populations. It should be emphatically stressed that all estimates of earlier populations except that recorded in the Bible (namely, that immediately after the great Flood, the world population consisted of eight people) are based solely on evolutionary concepts of human technological development.

> For still earlier periods (than A.D. 1) the population must be estimated indirectly from calculations of the number of people who could subsist under the social and technological institutions presumed to prevail at the time. Anthropologists and historians have estimated, for example, that before the introduction of agriculture the world would have supported a hunting and gathering culture of between five and ten million people.[15]

Such guesses are useless, however, because they are based on a discredited model, that of human evolution. The creation-cataclysm model of earth history fits all the known facts of man's history much better than the evolution model does, and it recognizes that man's agriculture and other basic technologies are essentially as old as man himself.

In 1650 the world population has been estimated with perhaps reasonable accuracy to have been 600 million. The average rate of increase for the period from 1650 to 1800, therefore, is this:

$$r = \left(\frac{10}{6}\right)^{\frac{1}{150}} - 1 = \frac{1}{3}\ \%$$

Since this period from 1650 and 1800 antedated the great advances in medicine and technology that have stimulated the more rapid population growth of the 19th and 20th centuries, and also since this is the

[14] A. J. Coale, "The History of the Human Population," *Scientific American*, vol. 231 (September 1974), p. 41.

[15] *Ibid.*

earliest period of time for which population data are at all reliable, it seems reasonable that this figure of 1/3 percent, rather than the 1/2 percent previously calculated, should be used as the norm for population growth throughout most of past history.

In that case, the length of time required for the population to grow from 2 people to one billion people, at 1/3 percent increase per year is indicated by the following calculation:

$$n = \frac{\log\left(\frac{10^9}{2}\right)}{\log(1.00333)} = 6{,}100 \text{ years}$$

To this should be added the 195 years since 1800. Therefore, the most probable date of man's origin, based on the known data from population statistics, is about 6,300 years ago.

This figure, of course, is vastly smaller than the usually assumed million year history of man. Nevertheless, it correlates well not only with biblical chronology, but also with other ancient written records as well as with even the usual evolutionary dates for the origin of agriculture, animal husbandry, urbanization, metallurgy, and other attributes of human civilization.

By arbitrary juggling of population models, of course, the evolutionist can manage to come out with any predetermined date he may choose. People should realize, however, that this *does* require an arbitrary juggling of figures, based solely on the assumptions of human evolution. The actual data of population statistics, interpreted and applied in the most conservative and most probable manner, point to an origin of the human population only several thousands of years ago. The present population could very easily have been attained in only about 6,000 years or so, even if the average population growth rate throughout most of history were only one-sixth as much as it is at present. The burden of proof is altogether on evolutionists if they wish to promote some other population model.

The biblical model for population growth starts with eight people (Noah, his wife, his three sons, and their wives) right after the great Flood. The date of the Flood is not certain. The Ussher Chronology dates it at about 2350 B.C., but possible gaps in the genealogies of Genesis 11 may justify a date as far back as, say, about 6000 B.C., with the probabilities favoring the lower limit rather than the upper limit.

Even using the short Ussher chronology, it is quite reasonable, as we have seen, for the population to have grown from 8 people to 5 billion people in 4,350 years. This growth represents an average annual increase of about 0.5 percent, or an average doubling time of 140 years. Such figures are quite consistent with all known data of population statistics, especially in the light of the fact that the human death rates were very low for many centuries after the Flood, and family sizes quite large. Thus, in all likelihood, the population growth was very substantial in the early centuries, at least as great as it has become in the present century. In turn, this means that the rate of increase may have been much *less* than 0.50 percent during the long period in between.

In any case, the conclusion is well justified that the biblical chronology, even in its most conservative form, fits well into all the known facts of population growth, much more so than does the evolutionary chronology of human history!

Life on Other Worlds

One very bizarre aspect of the New Age movement is the explosive rise of various forms of occultism in recent years. Such phenomena as "channeling" (the modern euphemism for spiritism or — better — demonism), witchcraft, and astrology are booming.

All of these are, not surprisingly, evolutionary religions, for they all reject the biblical God of creation. One of the founders and leading theoreticians of modern spiritism, for example, was Alfred Russel Wallace, whose better-known mark of distinction was his simultaneous "discovery" with Charles Darwin of "natural selection" as the supposed mechanism of evolution. In common with all other New Age cults, these are pantheistic evolutionary systems, rather than Darwinist systems, but they are just as passionately committed to some form of evolutionism, worshipping nature as "creator." As noted earlier, the influential Cambridge biologist Rupert Sheldrake, presents that view thus:

> But today, with the rise of the green movement, Mother Nature is reasserting herself, whether we like it or not. In particular, the acknowledgment that our planet is a living organism, Gaia, Mother Earth, strikes a responsive chord in millions of people; it reconnects us both with our personal, intuitive experience of nature and with the traditional understanding of nature as alive.[16]

This belief in pantheistic evolution applies today not only to Mother Earth, but to the entire cosmos itself. This belief is involved in astrology, of course, which is a way of rationalizing the idea that the stars and constellations are, in some sense, alive, and thus able to influence

[16] Rupert Sheldrake, *The Rebirth of Nature: The Greening of Science and of God* (New York, NY: Bantam Books, 1991), p. 10.

human lives and destinies. It also seems to justify the burgeoning belief in "aliens" or "extra-terrestrials," and their ability to travel from their worlds to our world in what we have called "unidentified flying objects," or "UFO's."

There is not one iota of scientific or biblical evidence that life exists anywhere else in the universe (with the exception, of course, of angels). The "evidence" is entirely anecdotal — tales of UFO sightings and kidnappings and the like — but there is an abundance of this kind of hearsay evidence, for what it is worth.

In view of the complete absence of any real scientific evidence of extra-terrestrial life, it is remarkable that many atheistic scientists (e.g., Carl Sagan) seem quite confident that many inhabited worlds do exist throughout the cosmos, with life forms comparable to those on Earth.

The complete absence of evidence for such life in outer space, however, is altogether ignored by those who believe in it. It is simply an article of faith that, since life has supposedly evolved on one planet in this solar system, it must also have evolved on planets in other solar systems. NASA scientists, especially the geologists associated with this country's space program, have always admitted that the main purpose of the program was to find evidence as to how this solar system evolved and also to try to find proof of life existing in other "worlds" within the universe.

This aspect of NASA's program, of course, proved to be a failure. There was no life on the moon, nor on any other planet in the solar system, exactly as predicted by creationists all along.

Furthermore, there is no observational evidence of any other planets anywhere else in the universe! Astronomers believe that there are millions of them, of course, but this idea is based squarely on evolutionary statistics! No one has ever actually *seen* any other planets, and science is supposed to be based on sight, not faith.

Astronomers have occasionally found evidence of molecules in space that are also found in living materials, and they have jumped to the conclusion that this somehow proves that evolution has occurred "out there," as well as on earth. Such a conclusion is hardly justified by the evidence, however. "Space" molecules are immensely short of being *living* molecules! Furthermore, even these cannot exist very long, and so could hardly evolve into higher molecules.

> Although it is clear that these molecules (e.g., OH, H_2, NH_3, H_2CO, HCN, CN HC_3N) exist in space and that they can emit radiation, there is no clear explanation of how they are formed and why they remain stable. Their

> chemical bonds should be broken by the intense fluxes of ultra-violet radiation and cosmic rays. Their estimated lifetimes from ultraviolet dissociation in interstellar space is about 200 years.[17]

Speculation seems to be unhindered by such facts, however. Many eminent evolutionist scientists continue to believe that life *must* be out there somewhere, because it would be improbable that it would evolve only once in the entire universe!

> They hypothesize that thousands of millions of years ago, an intelligent civilization decided to seed other nearby planets with primitive forms of life in the hope that more advanced civilizations might develop. Crick and Orgel claim that their proposal — called Directed Panspermia — is as tenable as other theories that aim to explain the origin of life on earth.[18]

If that be so, why then do we not find *some* evidence of intelligent life in other parts of the universe? A remarkable theory suggests that this is because the celestial astronauts do not want us to know that they are there!

> A humble explanation of the null results of the searches for life is advanced by a Harvard student, John Ball.[19] He steps into the realms of science fiction with a hypothesis that we are living in a galactic zoo! The idea is that a super civilization may by now have control of the whole galaxy. Just as we have safari parks, zoos and conservation areas, so they may have set aside the solar system as a wilderness zone. The perfect zoo keeper does not make himself known to his charges, and thus we are unaware of their presence.[20]

Since there is no evidence of life in outer space, so the argument goes, therefore it *must* be there! This kind of evidence is, to say the least, not compelling evidence! Nevertheless if men do not believe in a divine Creator, they must eventually believe in some kind of spontaneous generation of life. Such an idea as that, of course, clearly

---

[17] Gerald L. Wick, "Interstellar Molecules: Chemicals in the Sky," *Science*, vol. 170 (October 9, 1970), p. 1295.

[18] Simon Mitton and Roger Lewin, "Is Anyone Out There?" *New Scientist* (August 16, 1973), p. 380.

[19] John Ball, *Icarus*, vol. 19, p. 347.

[20] Simon Mitton and Roger Lewin, "Is Anyone Out There?" p. 382.

contradicts the scientific law of cause and effect.

As far as the evidence of high technological skills found in ancient structures and drawings is concerned, this in no way proves that these skills were imported from somewhere in outer space. To the extent that such evidences are genuine, they can be much more easily and directly explained in terms of the creation model, which suggests that the earliest men, being highly intelligent and living to great ages, had developed a very high civilization, both before the great Flood and, at least in many places, again quite soon after the Flood.

The creation model alone has a scientifically defensible explanation for life. It was specially created by the living Creator, who, himself, has existed from eternity. This explanation is perfectly consistent with causality and with all *known* data. And, as far as we can tell, biological life is unique to this earth.

Nevertheless, evolutionists keep on believing in extra-terrestrial life, and this is almost as true of materialistic evolutionists as of occultic evolutionists. Moreover, many Christians are enamored of the idea, even though the Bible makes it very plain that only "the earth hath [God] given to the children of men" (Ps. 115:16). It is only on planet Earth that God in Christ lived and died and rose again, and it is only here that He will reign forever over the cosmos.

Amazingly though, many scientists have seriously proposed that life evolved in outer space and then somehow reached the earth. Sir Fred Hoyle is one of these. Two other notable scientists, Sir Francis Crick (co-discoverer of DNA) and Leslie Orgel of the University of California at San Diego, have promoted the curious notion of "directed panspermia" (life-sperms are everywhere in space, and some have been directed by advanced galactic civilizations to the earth!), and this idea is receiving serious attention and wide acceptance. Both Orgel[21] and Crick[22] have made calculations and strong statements about the impossibility of chance origin of life on earth. Crick says this, for example:

> If a particular amino acid sequence was selected by chance, how rare an event would this be? . . . Suppose the chain is about two hundred amino acids long; this is, if anything, rather less than the average length of proteins of all types. Since we have just twenty possibilities at each place, the number of possibilities is twenty multiplied by

---

[21] Leslie Orgel, "Darwinism at the Very Beginning of Life," *New Scientist* (April 15, 1982), p. 149-152.

[22] Sir Francis Crick, *Life Itself* (New York, NY: Simon and Schuster, 1981).

> itself some two hundred times. This is approximately equal to . . . a one followed by 260 zeros. . . . The great majority of sequences can never have been synthesized at all, at any time.[23]

Sir Francis then makes the following fascinating admission:

> An honest man, armed with all the knowledge available to us now, could only state that in some sense, the origin of life appears at the moment to be almost a miracle, so many are the conditions which would have had to have been satisfied to get it going.[24]

But since he believes neither in God nor miracles, the eminent Dr. Crick opted for directed panspermia (more recently, he has backed off somewhat from this notion). There is, of course, not the slightest evidence anywhere (except in science fiction and various occult religions) of directed panspermia or anything else approximating extra-terrestrial human or animal life. The entire notion brings us once again to the threshold of an esoteric Marxism. Yockey phrases that view thus:

> Faith in the infallible and comprehensive doctrines of dialectic materialism plays a crucial role in origin of life scenarios, and especially in exobiology and its ultimate consequence, the doctrine of advanced extra-terrestrial civilization. That life must exist somewhere in the solar system or "suitable planets elsewhere" is widely and tenaciously believed in spite of lack of evidence, or even abundant evidence to the contrary.[25]

The extraordinary weakness — in fact complete absence — of any scientific evidence for a naturalistic origin of life anywhere in the universe is a well-kept secret of our establishment science, education, and news media. Christians need to know this fact — and use this fact — in their testimony to the world. It will be enlightening and effective in many hearts.

In a review article on this whole matter of the evolution of life in other worlds, as well as here on earth, John Horgan says:

---

[23] Sir Francis Crick, *Life Itself* (New York, NY: Simon and Schuster, 1981), p. 51.

[24] *Ibid.*, p. 88.

[25] H. P. Yockey, "Self-Organization Origin of Life Scenarios and Information Theory," *Journal of Theoretical Biology*, vol. 91 (1981), p. 27. Yockey is an evolutionary biochemist.

> About a decade ago Orgel and Crick managed to provoke the public and their colleagues by speculating that the seeds of life were sent to the earth in a spaceship by intelligent beings living on another planet. Orgel says that the proposal, which is known as directed panspermia, was "sort of a joke." But he notes that it had a serious intent: to point out the inadequacy of all explanations of terrestrial genesis.[26]

It was once fervently hoped and believed by evolutionary geologists and astronomers that the NASA space probes would find evidence of life, perhaps on the moon, and certainly on Mars. This hope, of course, proved futile, just as many of us had predicted — not because we were prophets, but simply because of biblical revelation concerning the divinely intended roles of the stars and planets in relation to Earth. Although a few evolutionists still hope against hope that some evidence of at least former life will be found on Mars, most now admit that this won't happen.

> Even though some ambiguities remain, there is little doubt about the meaning of the observations of the Viking landers: at least those areas on Mars examined by the two spacecraft are not habitats of life.[27]

No one really expected to find life on Saturn or Venus or any of the other planets, since the physical conditions on them are not amenable to life in any form. Consequently, the hopes of evolutionists now focus on planetary systems around other stars. Even if such stellar planetary systems do exist somewhere, however (and *this* has not yet been proved), it is futile to hope that any earthbound space probe will ever reach them. In reviewing a book by Isaac Asimov, John Emsley acknowledges the futility of that fantasy:

> Asimov also disposes of another popular myth — that one day we will journey to the stars. Here he is tampering with something that might have been better left alone. He quietly knifes the idea in the back, and thereby murders much popular culture on which today's young people are raised. Space travel is possible between the planets of the

[26] John Horgan, "In the Beginning," *Scientific American*, vol. 264 (February 1991), p. 125.

[27] Norman H. Horowitz, "The Search for Life on Mars," *Scientific American*, vol. 237 (November 1977), p. 61. Horowitz is biology department chairman at Cal Tech.

> solar system, but that is all. Whatever probe we launch from planet Earth into the cosmos will get nowhere. It will slowly come to rest between here and the next star. A manned spacecraft would suffer the same fate.[28]

Even if a spaceship could ever reach the nearest star, which is four light years from Earth, over 10,000 times farther away than the sun, Asimov has shown that such space travelers would require 50,000 years to get there and back!

> Because we can never visit another star, so we can never be visited by aliens from another Solar System. Another chunk of popular science folklore bites the dust. Space travel is a meaningless phrase. Star Wars, Star Trek, and a lot of science fiction suddenly seems merely silly. Asimov, you're a spoilsport![29]

Interestingly enough, Isaac Asimov wrote many books of science fiction dealing with life in other worlds. As a scientist, however, he realized that it was *fiction*! It could never be anything else, as far as our earthly lives are concerned. Asimov may have wished otherwise, for he himself was an atheistic humanist.

Most "exobiologists," as such scientists call themselves, now realize that they will never find *direct* evidence of life anywhere else in the universe. Accordingly, they now are hoping to find *indirect* evidence by listening to electromagnetic signals sent earthward by possible living beings out there. They have persuaded the government to waste great amounts of money in building and manning large radio-telescopes and other equipment that *might* be able to receive such signals. This pie-in-the-sky has also proved futile so far, and the government is about to give up such expensive evolutionizing.

> Is it still reasonable to be optimistic about the search for extra-terrestrial intelligence? After all, researchers around the world have been listening for electromagnetic signals from other civilizations in the universe for more than 25 years now, using ever larger telescopes and increasingly sophisticated equipment. Tipler (1987) estimates that 120,000 hours of observing time have been

---

[28] John Emsely, "Demolisher of Myths," review of *The Relativity of Wrong*, by Isaac Asimov (New York, NY: Oxford University Press, 1988.), in *New Scientist*, vol. 122 (April 8, 1989), p. 60.

[29] *Ibid.*

spent on the search, with, of course, no positive results.[30]

In spite of all the negative results in the search for signs of extra-terrestrial life, it *must* be there, because consistent evolutionary philosophy requires it!

> The basic argument for an optimistic assessment of the likelihood of intelligence elsewhere in the universe is really a reassertion of the ancient belief in the plurality of worlds, the idea that our own world must be duplicated elsewhere. In modern form, the idea assumes that, in the absence of evidence to the contrary, conditions favorable to the emergence of life and intelligence as they exist here on earth are present abundantly in the universe.[31]

Among the perennial optimists in this matter of extra-terrestrial life, the eminent astronomer Carl Sagan stands out. He was very positive in predicting life on Mars and is still hopeful that radio astronomy will turn up this missing evidence. In a recent review article, Sagan acknowledges that the results so far have been negative, but he is nevertheless "encouraged."

> While no one yet has found living organisms beyond the earth, there are reasons to be encouraged.[32]

Dr. Sagan's encouragement now centers on the hope that other solar systems like ours will someday be discovered (none have yet, of course), and the fact that organic molecules (meaning compounds that contain carbon) have been found in space. One must admit that Dr. Sagan does not get discouraged easily! It is hard for an atheist to acknowledge that planet Earth was uniquely created for life by the God who created all things, and that life was uniquely created for planet Earth. That, however, is exactly what all the factual scientific data indicate, and that is what the Bible teaches! Since science can never prove a universal negative, however, evolutionists will continue to have blind faith that life *must* have evolved in more than one place (planet Earth) in an almost infinite universe.

---

[30] David Schwartzman and Lee J. Rickard, "Being Optimistic about the Search for Extraterrestrial Intelligence," *American Scientist*, vol. 76 (July/August 1988), p. 364.

[31] *Ibid.*

[32] Carl Sagan, "The Search for Extra-Terrestrial Life," *Scientific American*, vol. 271 (October 1994), p. 93.

Chauvinism, Feminism, and Evolution

Traditional Darwinian evolution (slow and gradual struggle for existence and survival of the fittest), as applied in Social Darwinism, racism, imperialism, and fascism, is encountering hard times today, though evolutionism itself is as popular as ever. Now, however, punctuationism is increasingly in vogue. This fits better with Marxism, anarchism, and all the New Age evolutionary cults. And now Darwinism is being increasingly attacked by the modern feminist movement, led by women who resent the traditional inferior evolutionary status accorded them by the Darwinians. This is hardly surprising when one reads the statements on this subject by Charles Darwin and many of his followers.

Having already been labeled racists and imperialists by the new wave of Marxian "revolutionary evolutionists," who insist that the old-style slow-and-gradual evolution must be replaced by rapid-and-catastrophic evolution, Darwinists have now been labeled as chauvinistic and sexist by radical feminists as well.

In a popular book entitled *Darwin*, Wilma George has attacked Charles Darwin's theories of the effect of "sexual selection" on human evolution as not having any basis in scientific fact at all, but as having been based on his Victorian prejudices against women and their abilities. Darwin's own wife, Emma, was quite religious and found her husband's anti-religious views very painful and his incessant hypochondria (which some writers maintain was a psychoneurosis related to his anti-religious guilt feelings) very demanding, but nevertheless she was dutifully attentive and submissive to him throughout his life. Wilma George even shows that Darwin's insistence on an evolution-based male superiority was one major reason why he was able to get evolution so rapidly accepted in place of divine creation. Eveleen Richards comments on this as follows:

> In a period when women were beginning to demand the suffrage, higher education and entrance to middle-class professions, it was comforting to know that women could never outstrip men; the new Darwinism scientifically guaranteed it. . . . Darwinism supposedly proved female inferiority by "an evolutionary reconstruction that centers on the aggressive, territorial, hunting male and relegates the female to submissive domesticity and the periphery of the evolutionary process."[33]

---

[33] Eveleen Richards, book review in *New Scientist*, vol. 100 (December 22/29, 1983), p. 887.

The feminist movement is not attacking evolution *per se*, of course, but only Darwinian-style evolution, just as the modern Marxist evolutionists are doing.

As is evident, Charles Darwin, once considered such a great man and great scientist, is rapidly becoming little more than a fallen idol today, even to many who paid devoted homage to him just a few years ago.

Christian women should not be deceived by the radical feminist movement today, although women in these movements do have some legitimate complaints against a social system that still reflects in considerable degree the Social Darwinism of the post-Darwin century, as well as the evolutionary pantheism of both ancient and modern non-Christian religions and philosophies. Women who serve the Lord should remember that *all* of these other religious systems have relegated women to a very inferior place in society. As already pointed out, all such religions are fundamentally evolutionary philosophies of one sort or another.

The Bible, on the other hand, has never taught male "superiority," though it does delineate the distinctive divine purposes for men and women (a subject beyond the scope of this discussion). As far as "equal rights" are concerned, in terms of real eternal values, men and women have always been equal before God — equal in creation and equal in salvation.

> So God created man in his own image, in the image of God created He him; male and female created He them" (Gen. 1:27).
>
> There is neither male nor female; for ye are all one in Christ Jesus" (Gal. 3:28).

The real answer to the unresolved needs and problems of women in our society is an all-out commitment to genuine biblical creationism, and to the entire Scripture as the Word of God for the temporal and eternal life and happiness of mankind.

Darwin and others of his persuasion made much of what he called "sexual selection" as a key factor in evolution. He argued that evolutionary pressures had made males intellectually superior, as well as physically larger and stronger, in comparison to women.

> The chief distinction in the intellectual powers of the two sexes is shown by man's attaining to a higher eminence in whatever he takes up, than can women — whether requiring deep thought, reason, or imagination, or merely

the use of the senses and hands.[34]

A modern feminist writer, Bettyann Kevles, in an in-depth study of the teachings of Darwin and other evolutionists on supposed female inferiority as related to their evolutionary history, wrote as follows concerning an evolutionist contemporary of Darwin, George Romanes:

> Romanes . . . shared Darwin's view that females were less highly evolved than males — ideas which he articulated in several books and many articles that influenced a whole generation of biologists.[35]

Another modern evolutionist, Stephen Jay Gould, in a review of this rather sensitive subject, refers to the teachings of an influential 19th century surgeon and anthropologist, Paul Broca, founder of the Anthropology Society in Europe. Broca, with extensive data, concluded that the average female brain was significantly smaller than the average male brain, and that this proved the intellectual inferiority of women. Broca concluded that this was "a result of differing evolutionary pressures upon dominant men and passive women."[36]

Gould also noted:

> Broca's conclusions were the shared assumptions of most successful white males during this time.[37]

In another article, Gould quotes from Darwin's *Descent of Man* as follows:

> [Darwin says]: "It is generally admitted that with woman the powers of intuition, of rapid perception, and perhaps of imitation, are more strongly marked than in man; but some, at least, of these faculties are characteristic of the lower races, and therefore of a past and lower state of civilization."
>
> It is remarkable that Darwin manages to display his evolutionism, his racism, and his male chauvinism in just one sentence.[38]

---

[34] Charles Darwin, *The Descent of Man* (New York, NY: Appleton, 1896), p. 564.

[35] Bettyann Kevles, *Females of the Species* (Cambridge, MA: Harvard University Press, 1986), p. 8. Cited in "Darwin's Teaching of Women's Inferiority," *ICR Impact*, no. 249 (March 1994), p. i, by Dr. Jerry Bergman.

[36] Stephen Jay Gould, *The Mismeasure of Man* (New York, NY: W. W. Norton and Co., 1981), p. 104. Cited by Bergman, "Darwin's Teaching of Women's Inferiority," p. iii.

[37] Gould, *The Mismeasure of Man*, p. 85.

[38] Stephen Jay Gould, "The Moral State of Tahiti—and of Darwin," *Natural History* (October 1991), p. 14, quoting from Darwin's *Descent of Man*, 1896 ed., p. 564.

Darwin goes on to display still further his evolutionary prejudice against women.

> It is, indeed, fortunate that the law of the equal transmission of characters to both sexes has commonly prevailed throughout the whole class of mammals; otherwise it is probable that man would have become as superior in mental endowment to woman, as the peacock is in ornamental plumage to the peahen.[39]

With such an evolution-based attitude so prominent among men of the century following Darwin, it is at least understandable that there should develop a strong female revulsion against such male chauvinism. The result, however, has been a pagan feminist religion.

The consequent radical modern feminism is far more than an attempt by women to gain equal status with men in business and the professions. It is a drive to restore what many believe was once a matriarchal society, structured around the so-called "old religion," worshipping the goddess, essentially the same as Mother Earth, or Mother Nature.

Though the modern feminist movement tends to resent Darwin and the neo-Darwinian evolutionists, it has by no means abandoned evolutionism. All of its leaders, and most of its followers, are evolutionary humanists of the New Age variety, and their evolutionism is in general an updated pantheism, centered in the "goddess."

A significant minority are even involved in wicca, or witchcraft, which is alleged by its practitioners to be essentially a revival of the "Old Religion," practiced by ancient matriarchal societies before the rise of male dominance.

> They call themselves followers of the Craft or the Old Religion or wicca. They have nothing to do with either black magic or Christianity or, for that matter, with any monotheistic religion, as they are Neo-pagans. Some wiccans believe their gods — the lord of animals, of death and beyond, and the triple goddess (maiden, mother, and crone) — are through forms built up over the centuries. Others think they are archetypes, still others that they are literal divine entities. Whatever their understanding of the deities, these witches seek harmony with nature and to enhance their spiritual life.[40]

---

[39] *Ibid.*

[40] Derk Kinnone Roelofsma, "Inside the Circle of Witches Modern," *Insight* (June 8, 1987), p. 59.

There are believed to be only about 100,000 practicing witchcraft ("wise craft," or wicca) in the United States, but its origins are quite ancient.

> The Craft, the story goes, dates back to Paleolithic times when humans worshipped a goddess of fertility and a god of the hunt. The names of the deities changed from place to place, but basically the same gods were held in belief everywhere.[41]

This obviously is essentially ancient pagan occultism, or evolutionary pantheism, revived. There are many other groups of feminists, of course, and all believe in some form of evolutionism.

> Wicca devotees are not the only women to have rediscovered the Goddess. She has become the sacral element of the feminist movement, its binding spiritual force. Congregations of Woman Church abound. . . . Goddess devotees are at pains to emphasize a common creed of non-violence, care for the earth, and harmony of all things with nature.[42]

However, ordinary women, even those striving hard for elimination of sexism and for attainment of full equality with men, do not get very much involved with the actual theory and ritual of goddess worship.

> Constituents of the Goddess are, more often than not, academics, professionals, members of the highly educated elite. They talk a lot, they argue and dissent, they are keenly attuned to slight. . . . The Goddess of feminism (in whatever form) was rescued from oblivion to emblemize and sanctify the quest for woman-power in the private as in the political arena. And the evocation of a Golden Goddess Age lent the quest scholarly warrant. Ultimately, the Goddess is not for the many but for the self-chosen few. She is not a divinity for all seasons. It is hard to believe she ever was.[43]

Feminists occasionally argue that the Bible discriminates against women, but the fact is that Christian women in Christian homes in Christian countries are better treated and regarded more highly than are

---

[41] Derk Kinnone Roelofsma, "Inside the Circle of Witches Modern," *Insight* (June 8, 1987), p. 60.

[42] Olivia Vlahos, "The Goddess that Failed," *First Things* (December 1992), p. 12.

[43] *Ibid.*, p. 19.

any other women in the world. Women in pantheistic nations (e.g., India) are notoriously ill-treated, almost like slaves.

The Bible does indicate, of course, that God ordained distinctive roles for men and women, and they are physiologically equipped for those roles. Both sexes, however, are equal before the Lord, as far as worth and destiny are concerned. "For ye are all the children of God by faith in Christ Jesus. . . . there is neither male nor female: for ye are all one in Christ Jesus" (Gal. 3:28). Both men and women are "heirs together of the grace of life" (1 Pet. 3:7).

Evolutionary Dominance in Education

The current revival of interest in creationism has focused largely on the public schools. Parents, pastors, and others have become painfully aware that, in the name of "science," their young people are being thoroughly indoctrinated in the deadly philosophy of evolutionary humanism. Biblical creationism is either ridiculed or (which is even worse) ignored as not worth mentioning.

This indoctrination is accomplished not only formally and directly in, say, biology and geology courses, but even more effectively through indirect application of evolutionary assumptions in the social sciences and humanities, as well as in the very methodology of modern educationism. Occasionally, an educator will react defensively to such charges by insisting that, in his class or school, evolution is presented only as a "theory" and that other theories are also included. What this usually means is that various mythological ideas of origins are mentioned rapidly in passing (Hindu, American Indian, Babylonian, etc., as well as the "story" in Genesis), and then the rest of the semester is spent in studying the only "theory" that is taken seriously by *scientists* — namely, evolution!

One of the leading evolutionists of our times, Dr. Theodosius Dobzhansky, made a fascinating comment and admission in one of his seemingly innumerable articles, more than 30 years ago:

> It would be wrong to say that the biological theory of evolution has gained universal acceptance among biologists or even among geneticists. This is perhaps unlikely to be achieved by any theory which is so extraordinarily rich in philosophic and humanistic implications. Its acceptance is nevertheless so wide that its opponents complain of inability to get a hearing for their views.[44]

---

[44] Theodosius Dobzhansky, "Evolutionary and Population Genetics," *Science*, vol. 142 (November 29, 1963), p. 1134.

Note that evolution is "rich in philosophic and humanistic implications." It is those very implications to which creationists object. Moreover, this fact of an implied philosophy of humanism is exactly what brands evolution as fundamentally a *religion*, rather than a science!

When creationists propose, however, that creation be taught in the schools along with evolution, evolutionists commonly react emotionally, rather than scientifically. Their "religion" of naturalism and humanism has been, in effect, the established religion of the state for a hundred years, and they fear competition. They usually refuse to teach scientific creationism on the basis of their obviously false claim that creation is religion and evolution is science.

In the ultimate sense, *no* concept of origins can be really scientific. In the present world, neither evolution nor creation is taking place, so far as can be observed (and science is supposed to be based on observation!). Cats beget cats and fruit flies beget fruit flies. Life comes only from life. There is nothing new under the sun.

Neither evolution nor creation is accessible to the scientific method, since both deal with origins and history, not with presently observable and repeatable events. They can, however, be formulated as scientific *models*, or frameworks, within which to predict and correlate observed facts. Neither can be *proved*; neither can be *tested*. They can only be *compared* in terms of the relative ease with which they can explain data that exist in the real world.

There are, therefore, sound scientific and pedagogical reasons why *both* models should be taught, as objectively as possible, in public classrooms, giving arguments pro and con for each. Some students and their parents believe in creation, some in evolution, and some are undecided. If creationists desire *only* the creation model to be taught, they should send their children to private schools that do this; if evolutionists want only evolution to be taught, they should provide private schools for *that* purpose. The public schools should be neutral and either teach both theories or teach neither theory.

This is clearly the most equitable and constitutional approach. Many people have been led to believe, however, that court decisions restricting "religious" teaching in the public schools apply to "creation" teaching, and not to "evolution" teaching. Nevertheless, creationism is actually a far more effective scientific model than evolutionism, and evolution requires a far more credulous religious faith in the illogical and unprovable than does creation. An abundance of sound scientific literature is available today to document this statement, but few evolutionists have bothered to read any of it. Many of those who *have* read it have become creationists!

For a while, during the 1970s especially, evolutionists seemed willing to debate creationists on the scientific merits of evolution versus creation. These debates were commonly held in secular university or public high school auditoriums, with audiences largely composed of students, parents, and faculty. ICR scientists alone, especially Dr. Duane Gish, have participated in over 300 such debates. Almost invariably the creationists have won the debates, at least in the judgment of most of the audience.

Consequently, in recent years, it has become more difficult to arrange debates, particularly with eminent scientists. For example, such evolutionary spokesmen as Carl Sagan, Stephen Jay Gould, Isaac Asimov, and others of like prestige have never condescended to debate a creationist scientist. These men are, of course, quite prolific with bombastic statements about the unscientific nature of creationist arguments, as long as they can make such statements to sympathetic news reporters or to captive audiences in their classes.

In such debates as *are* scheduled, however, evolutionists will commonly attack the credentials or character of their opponents (*ad hominem* arguments), attack biblical statements (especially relative to the young earth and the global Flood), criticize fundamentalists in general and (perhaps) present some scientific evidence for micro-evolution (that is, horizontal variations *within* kinds). One thing that they *never* do is give any real scientific proof of *macro*-evolution. This they cannot do, of course, because no such proof exists — not even any good evidence!

The impact of the debates can be gauged by the concern shown by the evolutionists. A letter to the editor of *Bioscience* is indicative.

> Why do creationists seem to be the consistent winners in public debates with evolutionists? . . . We biologists are our own worst enemies in the creationist-evolutionist controversies. We must no longer duck this and other issues related to biology and human affairs, and when we do face them we must think clearly and express ourselves accordingly. We may still not be consistent winners in the creationist-evolutionist debates, but let the losses that occur be attributable to other than lapses in professional standards.[45]

---

[45] Dennis Dubay, "Evolution/Creation Debate," *Bioscience*, vol. 30 (January 1980), p. 4-5.

Much more vitriolic was an article by Joel Cracraft of the Department of Anatomy at the University of Illinois Medical Center in Chicago. Dr. Cracraft was a science advisor to the American Civil Liberties Union at the Arkansas Creation Trial of 1981, as well as organizer of an anti-creationist symposium at the 1981 convention of the American Association for Advancement of Science. Note, in the following, his backhanded admission of the rising influence of creationism, and the poor case that can be made for scientific evolutionism.

> With their pleas for a fair hearing, the scientific creationists, in particular those at the ICR, excel in duping the public and manipulating both the press and their adversaries. How else can one explain their countless speaking invitations from secular universities and the willingness of many scientists to debate them, as if "scientific" creationism were an intellectual equal of evolutionary biology or, more accurately, science as a whole?[46]

One could possibly explain this, Dr. Cracraft, by the fact that more and more people, especially college students, are becoming aware that they have, indeed, been duped for many years, though not by creationists. As Dr. Colin Patterson, one of the world's top evolutionists, said not long ago:

> Then I woke up and realized that all my life I had been duped into taking evolutionism as revealed truth in some way.[47]

It is most significant that Cracraft expresses strong objection to debating evolution and creation on their scientific merits:

> Debates are to the advantage of the creationists especially when they create the ground rules: "We will only debate the scientific evidences . . . religion and philosophy will not be subjects for discussion." . . . Structured in this way, debates invariably place scientists on the defensive because the creationists seek to promote a dualistic philosophy: evidence against evolution, they argue is evidence for creationism. On the other hand, it is no surprise

[46] Joel Cracraft, "Reflections on the Arkansas Creation Trial," *Paleobiology*, vol. 8, no. 2 (1982), p. 83.

[47] Colin Patterson, "Evolution and Creationism," Speech at American Museum of Natural History, transcript (New York, NY, November 5, 1981), p. 2.

> that creationists are reluctant to debate an altogether different proposition. Is "scientific" creationism science or religion?[48]

In other words, evolutionists would much rather attack the religious aspects of creationism than defend the scientific aspects of evolutionism! Creationists find it very difficult to understand why, if evolution is a proven fact of science (as evolutionists continually insist, and as they perpetually brainwash students into believing), that a debate argued strictly from the scientific evidence is "to the advantage of the creationists."

Concerning Cracraft's petty lament that creationists present only negative evidence against evolution, surely he is intelligent enough to realize that evidence against evolution, such as the creationists present in their lectures and debates, is, indeed, positive evidence for creation. *There are only these two possibilities!* Either all things have developed by natural processes in a self-contained universe, or at least some things have come by supernatural processes in an open universe. The one alternative is evolution, the other is creation, and there is no third option. In this type of debate, the creationist is not arguing against a particular form of evolution (e.g., neo-Darwinism), or for a particular account of creation (e.g., the Genesis record), but only the broad and basic question of whether observed scientific data fit evolution better than they fit creation.

For example, the evolution model would be strongly confirmed if one could find true transitional structures between major kinds of organisms, either in the fossil record or in living organisms (e.g., "sceathers," reptilian scales in the process of evolution into avian feathers). The creation model indicates that no such thing ever existed, since the Creator would have created fully functional structures for each creature in accordance with His intended purpose for that creature.

Therefore, the ubiquitous, unbridgeable gaps between major kinds of organisms constitute strong evidence (though not "proof") against evolution, and strong evidence (though not "proof") for creation. The same "dualism" (as Cracraft dubs it) will be found to apply to the other scientific arguments used by creationists (the Second Law of Thermodynamics, the deteriorative nature of mutations, the improbability of complex or symbiotic systems, the conservative character of natural selection, etc., etc.).

The debates have surely brought one important fact to the attention

[48] Joel Cracraft, "Reflections," p. 83-84.

of the public. Creationism can at least be discussed scientifically, strictly on the evidence from scientific data. Evolutionists may complain that creationists have a "hidden agenda," as the title of an article in the journal *Christianity Today* put it, and that they really believe in the biblical account of creation even though they don't talk about it in their debates. But this is all irrelevant to the basic question of whether the actual hard data of paleontology, genetics, thermodynamics, etc., fit in with the *scientific* model of creationism, *as well as or better than they fit in with evolution.* This is the only aspect of creationism that creationists believe should be taught in public institutions anyway, so this is the only aspect that should be debated in such institutions.

But evolutionists, intuitively realizing that any real scientific case for evolution is very weak (creationists would say that it is nonexistent!), prefer to defend it by branding creation as "religious," and then having creationism excluded from public institutions on the basis of church/state separation. A favorite tactic is to cite some creationist book or article expounding biblical creationism, and then to recoil with horror at the prospect of having *that* concept taught to public school children.

Cracraft, for example, has used this device. After quoting (out of context) one of our discussions on the subject of the possible influence of Satan, angels, and demons on earth and cosmic history (which are topics definitely treated in the Bible and even discussed in some detail by our Lord Jesus Christ) in a book specifically stated to be a Bible commentary, and certainly never intended for use in public schools, Cracraft then makes the following utterly irrelevant and cleverly misleading comment:

> Inasmuch as Dr. Morris and others like him want to exercise control over the public school curricula, those reading this should take it upon themselves to make Dr. Morris' judgments about science available to local school boards, religious leaders, and state legislators. After all, he is director of the most important creationist organization in the United States and will be directly involved in writing educational materials for the public schools if creationists get their way.[49]

Well, apparently all is fair in love and war, and evolutionists have definitely mounted a new war against creation.

Creationists in no way wish to *control* public school curricula, of

[49] Joel Cracraft, "Reflections on the Arkansas Creation Trial," *Paleobiology*, vol. 8, no. 2 (1982), p. 88.

course, but they *have* been urging school administrators to be fair and to use a "two-model" approach in the schools. Since there are only two real world views of origins, history and meaning (that is, God-centered or man-centered, creationism or evolutionism, theism or humanism), why should tax-supported institutions be used to brainwash impressionable students *only* in evolutionary humanism? The latter is certainly no more scientific, nor less religious, than theistic creationism.

Furthermore, the founding principles of our nation were based upon the truth of a Creator and of a natural order and moral law created by God. The Declaration of Independence itself begins with this premise. Dr. Elias Boudinot, president of the Continental Congress in 1782, in an Independence Day address that year, gave expression to what was commonly believed by Americans at that time:

> The history of the world, as well sacred as profane, bears witness to the use and importance of setting apart a day as a memorial of great events, whether of a religious or a political nature. No sooner had the great Creator of the heavens and the earth finished His almighty work, and pronounced all very good, but He set apart (not an anniversary, or one day in a year), but one day in seven, for the commemoration of His inimitable power in producing all things out of nothing.[50]

How, then, could it now be wrong to teach in our schools — at least as an alternative — the very premise upon which our nation and its government were founded? Dr. Boudinot, and most other American leaders of that day, even believed and taught *biblical* creationism (he was, in fact, also the first president of the American Bible Society). Some, as deists, did not believe in biblical inerrancy, but they did believe in God and creation. Even such a deist as Thomas Jefferson, often quoted as the great advocate of church-state separation, believed in special creation and rejected the evolutionary theories of his day.

Separation of church and state, incidentally, has never been a constitutional requirement, only a modern judicial interpretation. The First Amendment prohibited an "established religion," which, in the context of the times, meant only the state endorsement and support of a particular sect or denomination. It was certainly *never* intended to ban God from the schools and to establish the religion of secular humanism

---

[50] Elias Boudinot, "Independence Day Address," presented to the New Jersey Society of the Cincinnati, July 4, 1873. Cited in *Foundation for Christian Self-Government Newsletter* (July 1982), p. 3.

in our schools, as has been done.[51]

For that matter, hardly anyone would even argue that such was the original intent. The problem is that evolution has been applied to our legal system as well. Modern lawyers and judges, steeped in evolutionary philosophy in their training, have come to regard the Constitution as "evolving" along with society. There are no "absolutes" in an evolving world, so even the Constitution, as well as the Bible and the concept of God, must evolve along with the changing mores of the current times.

Accordingly, "liberal" justices have gradually banned not only sectarianism, but even Christianity itself from the classrooms of what the founding fathers had intended (and the Supreme Court had affirmed, more than once) to be a Christian nation, one that accepted the Bible as the authoritative Word of God. In the process, of course, classroom prayer and Bible reading have now also been outlawed in the public schools.

It was the hope of the creationist scientists that, by stressing the scientific validity of creationism and making it clear that they were not asking for the biblical version of creation to be taught in the schools, many teachers and school administrators would begin to take advantage of their constitutional rights (as well as those of their students), by using the scientific evidences and arguments that were now becoming more accessible, to begin a real "two-model" approach in the schools, thus being fair to both evolutionists and creationists among their constituents.

Much headway was being made along these lines, and more and more schools and teachers began to do just this. The various teacher-education programs of ICR, along with the literature now available, were becoming widely effective.

But the opposition began to grow as well, and progress seemed too slow to suit many impatient creationist activists. Deciding that their constitutional rights were being violated (as indeed they were), many decided to try the political route, initiating litigation and/or legislation to *compel* the schools and other public institutions to adopt a two-model approach. Lawsuits were filed in Washington, DC, Houston, Sacramento, and other places, and creationist bills were introduced in many legislative assemblies.

Despite widespread publicity to the contrary, the Institute for Creation Research had always tried to discourage a legalistic and political approach to this issue (as has the Creation Research Society).

---

[51] Wendell R. Bird, "Freedom from Establishment and Unneutrality in Public School Instruction and Religious School Regulation," *Harvard Journal of Law and Public Policy* (June 1979), p. 127-129, 138-140.

History shows that neither scientific nor religious principles can be effectively legislated, and since there had been no legal restriction against teaching creation anyway, most creationist scientists felt rather strongly that, in the long run, education and persuasion would accomplish more than legislation and coercion.

Furthermore, the present legal and judicial climate is so humanistic that court decisions, no matter how strong the evidence and how valid the constitutional position, commonly go against the creationists. Even in the event of a favorable court decision, the creationists always seem to lose the case in the biased reporting of the news media. Finally, such laws would be very difficult to enforce, even if passed and upheld by the courts. Teachers compelled to teach creationism against their will, and without any adequate knowledge of the creationist arguments and evidence, would probably do more harm than good in the classroom anyway.

So, although the route of persuasion seems slower than that of compulsion, it holds more promise of ultimate success, and our ICR literature has stressed this repeatedly. However, many creationists have felt otherwise and have tried to use the courts or legislatures to get the two-model approach accepted.

This situation placed ICR in a difficult position. While not favoring legislative or political action at all, poorly drawn bills and political defeats would prove so harmful that ICR inadvertently became involved in these activities to try to prevent damaging errors. For example, a model creation *resolution* (not *law*) was prepared by ICR in order to enable school boards to *encourage* (not *compel*) a two-model approach, and ICR scientists and attorneys have been allowed to go on temporary leave in order to serve as expert witnesses or deputized attorneys in connection with creationist litigation. The costs of all such activities were always borne not by ICR, but by the organizations requesting them.

The Arkansas creation law resulted, of course, in a lawsuit filed by the ACLU and, finally, a strongly negative decision striking down the bill. Even more harmfully, it resulted in a news-media circus and a great wave of bad publicity for the whole creationist cause. A similar ACLU lawsuit against a more secularized, but similar, law in Louisiana eventually reached the U.S. Supreme Court, where the evolutionists again won, though against a sharply reasoned dissent by Justices Scalia and Rehnquist.

In spite of the bad precedent set in Arkansas and Louisiana, one good result may have been accomplished. The tremendous publicity generated by these trials, coming on top of the increasing interest generated by creationist books, debates, seminars, and other activities, caused a sharp upturn in public awareness of the issue, and apparently even a significant increase of belief in creationism.

A Gallup poll in 1980 showed that over half the population of the United States believes in a literal, specially created Adam and Eve as the parents of the whole human race. Then a 1981 Associated Press-NBC News poll found that no less than 76 percent of the people wanted creation to be taught along with evolution in the public schools, and that another 10 percent wanted *only* creation to be taught! Then, in August 1982, another Gallup poll found that 44 percent of the people believed not only in creation, but in *recent* creation, less than 10,000 years ago. Thirty-eight percent *more* believed in God as Creator, though they believed in an old earth and a divinely guided process of evolution. Only 9 percent believed in atheistic evolution, and 9 percent were undecided.

These sampling statistics are especially significant in the light of the many decades of indoctrination through the schools, textbooks, and news media to the effect that the earth is billions of years old, total evolution is a scientific fact, and creationism, being purely religious, has no place in the schools. No wonder the evolutionists have become almost hysterical in their opposition to the creationist movement!

An interesting comment appeared following the Sacramento lawsuit of early 1981, filed by a creationist group (the Creation Science Research Center) against the state on the basis that exclusive evolutionary teaching in the schools was an infringement on their religious rights.

> For his own part, [attorney for the CSRC] Turner says his recent experience in the courtroom has whetted his desire for more. "These scientists get up on the stand, and act as if their very lives were being attacked. They not only close ranks, but they almost deny anybody the right to know the internal fights that go on within the evolutionary crowd. They're pompous and arrogant, just the kind of people that the First Amendment was written to protect us against."[52]

From personal experience in many debates, and with evolutionist questioners (and often hecklers) in many campus audiences, ICR scientists can unequivocally echo Mr. Turner's observations. If evolution is irrefutably scientific and objectively factual, as evolutionists have tried to persuade themselves, it is strange that they quickly become extremely

[52] William J. Broad, "Creationists Limit Scope of Evolution Case," *Science*, vol. 211 (March 20, 1981), p. 1332.

emotional and angry when any scientific question is raised about its validity. These are not appropriate attitudes and reactions for *scientists*!

The reality is, of course, that evolution is not a science at all, but a religion, and creationists are questioning the tenets of a fanatical religion. No wonder its devotees become hysterical!

The writers have discussed the essentially religious character of evolutionism in many other places,[53] so they will not do so here, except to note that evolutionists themselves are becoming very sensitive on this issue.

> A rallying of the ranks would definitely be needed if creationists argued that evolution was a religion. Constitutional scholars do not scoff at the issue, one expert at Harvard recently saying that it is "far from a frivolous argument."[54]

The evolutionary religion, of course, is simply humanism (at least as taught in American schools), and even the American Humanist Association acknowledges that humanism is "a non-theistic religion."

> The creationists have portrayed Darwinism as a cornerstone of "secular humanism," a term they use to describe the belief that man, not God, is the source of right and wrong. They blame humanist teaching for all sorts of modern ills — from juvenile delinquency to the high rate of abortions — and want to replace it with the teaching of Christian morality. . . . As the creationists' goals become clear, many scientists, realizing that they have been secular humanists all along, are beginning to marshal their forces. . . . Evolutionists are beginning to realize that, for the first time in half a century, they may have to defend themselves in court.[55]

Some sense of the alarm in the evolutionists' camp was indicated by a remarkable fund-raising letter circulated by the atheistic humanist Isaac Asimov, on behalf of the American Civil Liberties Union and its Louisiana creation lawsuit:

> We must be prepared for the long and costly battle of

---

[53] For example, *King of Creation* (San Diego, CA: Creation-Life Publishers, 1980), p. 67-108.

[54] William J. Broad, "Creationists Limit Scope," p. 1331.

[55] Joel Gurin, "The Creationist Revival," *The Sciences,* vol. 23 (New York Academy of Science, April 1981), p. 34.

> challenging every creationist statute in every state in which it is introduced. Unbelievable as it may seem, there are millions of Americans who call themselves "scientific creationists." These religious zealots . . . are marching like an army of the night into our public schools with their Bibles held high. . . . Today, I am writing my personal check for $100 to help the ACLU finance this important case. I urge you, too, to write your check today. Your help is needed desperately right now.[56]

Another interesting commentary on the state of mind of evolutionists was provided by Norman Macbeth. After first discussing an article refuting natural selection, written by Professor Ronald Brady, Macbeth narrates the following:

> A few minutes ago I mentioned Ron Brady's article on natural selection in *Systematic Zoology*. I will not name the man or the college in this case but it was an Ivy League College and a respectable man. . . . So they told [a student] to go on down to the library . . . and read it right there. He came back in half an hour and said, ". . . the article isn't there, it's been scissored out." Next day the assistant professor went into the office of the head of the department on some other business and on the head's table he saw the missing pages. . . . The head of the department said, "Well, of course I don't believe in censorship in any form, but I just couldn't bear the idea of my students reading that article." End of story.[57]

Macbeth, who was on close speaking terms with many leading evolutionists, especially in the northeastern states, noted that they were almost irrationally fearful of the creationists and were determined to stop them by any means possible. Furthermore, says Macbeth:

> They are not revealing all the dirt under the rug in their approach to the public. There is a feeling that they ought to keep back the worst so that their public reputation would not suffer and the creationists wouldn't get any ammunition.[58]

---

[56] Isaac Asimov, Fund Appeal Letter for American Civil Liberties Union (March 1982).
[57] Norman Macbeth, "Darwinism: A Time for Funerals," *Towards*, vol. 2 (Spring 1982), p. 22.
[58] *Ibid.*

Time and space do not allow us to survey the multitude of anti-creationist books and articles being published today. More than 50 books and almost every scientific and educational journal, most of the popular magazines, and most of the nation's newspapers have featured one or more anti-creationist articles in recent years. Practically all are characterized by gross misunderstanding at best and blatant falsehood at worst, presenting a distorted caricature of creationism and the creationist movement in general, and often attacking ICR and its scientific staff in particular.

The same false charges (long since answered) are repeated over and over, apparently on the principle that wishful thinking will make them valid. A large number of both local and national telecasts, as well as radio broadcasts, have likewise attempted to smear creationists. Always the theme is that creationists are nothing but a small group of religious fundamentalists attempting to force their unscientific views on other people, whereas evolutionists are careful, clear-thinking, sober-minded scientists.

But this media attack has not worked, and more and more people are becoming creationists. Not only the American Civil Liberties Union, but many other organizations became more and more active in anti-creationist propaganda. The most prestigious of all scientific organizations, the National Academy of Sciences, hosted a meeting in October 1981, with representatives from many key organizations[59] present, to plan a broad nationwide anti-creationist strategy for the years ahead.

The meeting produced many suggestions. A paper circulated among the participating societies by A. G. Lasen, executive director of Assembly of Life Sciences, National Academy of Sciences, after the meeting, presented a summary of its recommendations. Among these were the following:

> A communications network called Committees of Correspondence . . . to use political action at the local level.[60]

---

[59] Organizations included were the American Association for Advancement of Science, American Humanist Association, National Association of Biology Teachers, American Anthropological Association, National Science Teachers Association, American Museum of Natural History, Smithsonian Institution, American Society of Biological Chemists, National Cancer Institute, Biological Sciences Curriculum Study, American Geological Institute, American Institute of Biological Sciences, and others.

[60] Alvin G. Lazen, "Summary Report: Meeting on Creationism-Evolutionism," *National Academy of Sciences* (Washington, DC, October 19, 1981), p. 2.

These local committees had already been initiated by an activist group in the AAAS, and they have indeed become quite active in fighting creationism at the local level. Continuing with other recommendations, we note the following:

> It was generally agreed that debates were to be avoided. . . . However, it was recognized that debates might be unavoidable . . . and that it was necessary to find means to identify appropriate debaters and to better prepare them for their task. . . . It was suggested by several persons that an "Institute for Evolution Research" was needed to counter the San Diego-based Institute for Creation Research.[61]

There was much more, but a key paper was that presented by veteran creationist-fighter John A. Moore of the University of California at Riverside. Dr. Moore's long diatribe included at least a dozen major recommendations, many of them involving substantial costs. But first he made this very significant acknowledgment:

> The climate of the times suggests that the problem will be with us for a very long time. . . .[62]

One thing is sure: the situation will never revert to the way it was before, as evolutionists might wish. There are now thousands of fully qualified scientists who have become creationists, and there are many more thousands of creationist students in the universities and colleges. Almost half of the American population now believes in special, recent creation, notwithstanding decades of evolutionary brainwashing in the schools, and almost 90 percent want creation to be brought back into the public schools and taught as a viable model of origins. The evolutionists have good cause to be concerned; the creationists are no longer an insignificant fringe minority.

Dr. Moore went on to recommend that a national coalition of societies and universities be formed to fight creation. This national consortium would, among other things perform the following:

1. Establish a national information-gathering network,
2. Keep the scientific and educational establishments informed,

---

[61] *Ibid.*, p. 3.

[62] John A. Moore, "Countering the Creationists," paper presented to the National Academy of Sciences *Ad Hoc* Committee on Creationism (Washington, DC, October 19, 1981), p. 1.

3. Assemble anti-creationist statements and classroom materials,
4. Maintain a list of key individuals for different assignments,
5. Support travel and other costs of anti-creationist projects,
6. Secure cooperation of liberal church groups, social scientists, and others,
7. Obtain college funds from foundations and individuals,
8. Conduct anti-creationist short courses for teachers and others,
9. Reform scientific education to pre-empt creationist inroads,
10. Contact lawmakers and other people of key influence,
11. Encourage evolutionists to speak with force and authority,
12. Seek to persuade every American scientist and science teacher to contribute about $10 annually for the work of the consortium.

Dr. Moore concluded his paper with the following cogent warning and claim (sad to say, a true claim):

> If we do not resolve our problems with the creationists, we have only ourselves to blame. Let's remember, the greatest resource of all is available to us — the educational system of the nation.[63]

There have been a number of similar "war councils" and other meetings sponsored by various organizations in recent years. A group of scientists and others associated with the American Humanist Association started publishing a regular anti-creationist journal, and the National Biology Teachers Association publishes a regular anti-creationist newsletter. At least 50 bitter and misleading anti-creationist books have been published since 1970.

This horrendously costly and troublesome anti-creationist vendetta is, of course, all very unnecessary. Since evolution is presumably a fact of science, all the evolutionists need to do is to present one scientific *proof* of evolution. Or even some real unequivocal scientific evidence. *That* would stop the creationist movement cold! Why haven't they thought of that? Undoubtedly, they have, and their inability has only added to their frustration and fury.

---

[63] *Ibid.*, p. 6.

Games People Play

One leading evolutionary scientist has recently made a most revealing admission. Richard Dickerson, an authority in the esoteric field of chemical evolution, said this:

> Science, fundamentally, is a game. It is a game with one overriding and defining rule. Rule No. 1: Let us see how far and to what extent we can explain the behavior of the physical and material universe in terms of purely physical and material causes, without invoking the supernatural.[64]

Therefore, science (or at least evolutionary "science") is not necessarily a search for truth, as we used to be told, but a game in which scientists try to find naturalistic causes for all things, including even the origin of the universe and everything in it.

I still remember the remarkable statement of a professor in the audience at the conclusion of a creation/evolution debate in which I participated a number of years ago. He said, in effect: "You may well be right; special creation is probably the truth and evolution is wrong. Nevertheless, evolution is science, and creation is religion, so only evolution should be taught in schools." Not every evolutionist is as frank as this, but this really *is* the game they play!

A second rule seems to be that the end justifies the means. In Stephen Jay Gould's book *The Mismeasure of Man*, that noted evolutionary author argues that the sociopolitical bias of an author (Gould himself has admitted being a Marxist) could well have an effect on his scientific results. Commenting on this, another admitted evolutionary Marxist at Harvard, Dr. Richard Lewontin, has (no doubt subconsciously) suggested this second rule of the evolutionists' game plan:

> Scientists, like others, sometimes tell deliberate lies, because they believe that small lies can serve big truths.[65]

Even though scientists never cite any real scientific evidence for evolution, doctrinaire evolutionists insist that there *is* such evidence, because any alternative is outlawed by the rules of the game they are playing.

---

[64] Richard E. Dickerson, "The Game of Science," *Perspectives on Science and Faith*, vol. 44 (June 1992), p. 137.

[65] Richard C. Lewontin, "The Inferiority Complex," *New York Review of Books* (October 22, 1981).

> In other words, it's natural selection or a Creator. This is why prominent Darwinists like G. G. Simpson and Stephen Jay Gould, who are not secretive about their hostility to religion, cling so vehemently to natural selection. To do otherwise would be to admit the probability that there is design in nature — and hence a Designer.[66]

A third rule of this game of evolutionary science seems to be to insist that all scientists, by definition, are evolutionists. Even though there are today thousands of creationists with post-graduate degrees in science, who are pursuing professional careers in science, they are commonly ignored or ridiculed or even denied status as scientists at all, by the evolutionary establishment. The ploy is that, no matter what scientific credentials they might have, scientists cannot become creationists without forfeiting their status *as* scientists.

In fact, many think that it would be better not ever to let creationists become scientists at all! Many years ago, when one of us was an engineering department chairman at Virginia Tech, he asked the biology professor there in charge of the doctoral program in that department whether a creationist student could get a Ph.D. degree in his department. The answer was — flat out — "*No!*" No matter how outstanding his grades or his dissertation or even his knowledge of evolutionary theory might be, if he did not *believe* in evolution, he could not get the degree. That's the rule of the game!

This commitment to the rules has been expressed most starkly by two liberal Iowa professors:

> As a matter-of-fact, creationism should be discriminated against. . . . No advocate of such propaganda should be trusted to teach science classes or administer science programs anywhere or under any circumstances. Moreover, if any are now doing so, they should be dismissed.[67]

That "liberal" opinion was written by an Iowa State University engineering professor, and published by the main national organization dedicated to fighting creationism wherever it surfaces — an organization whose establishment was funded by the Carnegie Foundation. An even more "liberal" sentiment was expressed by another Iowa professor, who said that any professor should have the right to "fail any student in

[66] George S. Johnston, "The Genesis Controversy," *Crisis* (May 1989), p. 17.

[67] John Patterson, "Do Scientists and Educators Discriminate Unfairly Against Creationists?" *Journal of the National Center for Science Education* (Fall 1984), p. 19.

his class, no matter what the grade record indicates"[68] if that professor discovers that the student is a creationist. Furthermore, the student's department should have the right of "retracting grades and possibly even degrees"[69] if the student becomes a creationist later.

Two modern California cases illustrate how the game is currently played. In Vista, California, the school board, after an election, for the first time (1993) had a majority of Bible-believing Christians on the board. However, since this community had been selected for aggressive and innovative new programs for teaching evolution, much was at stake. Therefore, the evolutionists in the community proceeded to promote a recall election because of their groundless fear that the "fundamentalist-dominated" board might try to introduce creationism into science classes in their schools. The board had never moved to do any such thing, but, when evolutionists demanded the issue be brought to an immediate head, it had simply proposed that a non-evolutionary supplementary text, *Of Pandas and People*, be approved for reference use in biology classes. This book does not mention creation nor God and does not oppose evolution *per se*, but does argue that the intricate complexity of living creatures implies some kind of "intelligent design." The furor of the evolutionary contingent in the community, at even the *hint* that God somehow might have been involved in origins, was amazing to see!

Soon after that, a similar teapot-tempest blew in at San Francisco State University, where Dean Kenyon, one of the co-authors of the book *Of Pandas and People*, was a tenured professor. Dr. Kenyon had been teaching the standard course in evolution there for many years, and was a recognized authority on evolution, even having authored a widely used textbook arguing for the naturalistic origin of life. A number of years ago, however, he had become a creationist, partially through reading creationist books. When he came with his new book advocating "intelligent design," and especially after this book received such notoriety in Vista, his department chairman, supported evidently by the rest of the department, censured him and took his course away from him.

It was encouraging and surprising in this case, however, that the faculty senate at San Francisco State and even the American Association of University Professors partially supported Dr. Kenyon in this situation, contending that he was denied due process. Maybe there is still

---

[68] Kendrick Frazier, "Competence and Controversy," *Skeptical Inquirer*, vol. 8 (Fall 1983), p. 2-5.

[69] *Ibid.*

some slight hope that the rules of the game can be changed enough to incorporate academic freedom for creationist students and faculty in public institutions.

But don't count on it. Dr. Eugenie Scott, director of the National Center for Science Education, has made it clear that the evolutionary establishment not only opposes the teaching of biblical creationism in public schools and colleges, but also opposes "scientific creationism," "intelligent design," "abrupt appearance," or any other system that would dilute naturalistic evolution. They oppose allowing any arguments or evidence that might throw any doubt whatsoever on evolution. The name of the game is evolution, and *only* evolution, with no hint permitted of anything else.

Furthermore, evolutionism is not limited to science courses. The schools and their evolutionary leaders are engaged in a deadly game with very broad goals, and these social goals are all based on evolution.

The rules of this evolutionary game definitely do not include fair play for creationists, or for Christians in general. If the reigning naturalists continue to win, the prize will eventually be a world government controlled by a political, economic, and educational system grounded and built on evolutionary humanism.

Just before he died, the famous Christian scholar C.S. Lewis, who had long supported the idea of theistic evolution, changed his mind, and declared the following:

> I wish I were younger. What inclines me now to think you may be right in regarding [evolution] as the central and radical lie in the whole web of falsehood that now governs our lives is not so much your arguments against it as the fanatical and twisted attitudes of its defenders.[70]

This is, indeed, a lethal game that some people are playing! And they are playing it in deadly earnest for their team coach, the father of lies (see John 8:44).

---

[70] C. S. Lewis, private letter (1951) to Captain Bernard Acworth, one of the founders of the Evolution Protest Movement (England). Cited by Dr. Ronald Numbers in his book, *The Creationists* (Adolph Knoff Co., 1991), p. 153.

Chapter 6

Evolution and Compromising Christians

Although nothing is impossible with God, it would seem that our nation's public schools and secular universities are so completely dominated by evolutionary humanism and its evil fruit that they are almost beyond hope of reclamation, humanly speaking. This, of course, is the primary reason for the explosive growth of the Christian school movement and, more recently, the home school movement in this country in recent years.

This growth has been in spite of many legal challenges attempting to thwart it. So far, however, the courts have largely upheld the rights of Christian parents and teachers to establish such schools and to teach their curricula in a biblical and creationist framework.

One notable victory was in the federal lawsuit of the Institute for Creation Research Graduate School against California's State Department of Public Instruction, which had tried vigorously to shut it down for teaching its science graduate degree programs in a framework of scientific biblical creationism. The educational establishment, under Superintendent Bill Honig, had maintained that it was illegal to teach science, even in a private Christian school, unless it was done in terms of evolution. In 1992 however, the federal district judge in San Diego issued a declaratory judgment to the effect that ICR and all other private Christian schools were free to teach *any* subject in any context they might choose. So far, at least to our knowledge, this ruling has not been challenged.

Furthermore, despite much opposition, also in 1992, the secretary of education, Lamar Alexander, approved (on appeal) the recognition of the Transnational Association of Christian Colleges and Schools as an approved accreditation agency for creationist institutions of post-secondary education. As of 1995 TRACS has recognized at some level of membership over 60 such colleges and seminaries, including ICR's Graduate School.

Sadly, however, the creation movement today is beginning to receive almost as much opposition from compromising Christian individuals and organizations (churches, schools, publications, etc.) as from the evolutionary humanists. "Christian" compromise is nothing new, of course — especially on this issue — but it does seem to be gaining new momentum in recent years, just as creationism, ironically, is meeting with significant success in the *public* arena.

Theological Confusion

It is inexcusable for evolutionary scientists to accept evolution as a scientific fact, when all the *facts* of science conflict with evolution and support creation, but at least we can understand the humanist desire to find a naturalistic origin for everything. Evolutionists feel it to be the peculiar mission of science to explain all physical reality without God. Though we as Christian creationist scientists disagree with this idea, we can comprehend it.

But what can we say about those *theologians* who are evolutionists? Why should those whose specialty is "the study of God" (for that is what "theology" means) attempt to explain things *without God* (for that is what evolution purports to do)? Is this strange behavior occasioned because "they loved the praise of men more than the praise of God" (John 12:43)?

Such theologians apparently suppose that evolution may be God's method of creation, but this is a serious charge to bring against God! Evolution is the most wasteful, inefficient, cruel way that one could conceive by which to create man. If evolution *is* true, we certainly should not blame God for it!

The famous scientist-philosopher Bertrand Russell had some incisive comments to make about such evolutionist theologians in his well-known atheistic book *Religion and Science*:

> Religion, in our day, has accommodated itself to the doctrine of evolution, and has derived new arguments from it. We are told that "through the ages one increasing purpose runs," and that evolution is the unfolding of an idea which has been in the mind of God throughout. It appears that during those ages which so troubled Hugh Miller, when animals were

> torturing each other with ferocious horns and agonizing stings, Omnipotence was quietly waiting for the ultimate emergence of man, with his still more widely diffused cruelty. Why the Creator should have preferred to reach his goal by a process, instead of going straight to it, these modern theologians do not tell us. Nor do they say much to allay our doubts as to the gloriousness of the consummation.[1]

But can't we be *Christian* evolutionists, they say. Yes, no doubt it is possible to be a Christian *and* an evolutionist. Likewise, one can be a Christian thief, or a Christian adulterer, or a Christian liar! Christians can be inconsistent and illogical about many things, but that doesn't make them right.

We are thankful for the great numbers of godly theologians who are true to the Scriptures, as well as to the real facts of science, and who, therefore, are strong creationists. We are concerned and sad for those out-of-character theologues who are not.

One of the most significant aspects of the modern revival of creationism is that it was spearheaded by scientists rather than theologians. As a matter of fact, it is usually easier to convert a scientist to belief in creation, than it is to win a "liberal" theologian or philosopher. The latter are more committed to evolution than even evolutionary scientists! Scientists normally deal in facts, whereas liberal religionists, not being experienced in the factual approach to science, and having long since rejected the factuality of the Bible, are completely adrift on a sea of metaphysical speculation.

Such liberal theologues (as well as their compromising conservative colleagues) suppose that evolution is God's "method of creation," ignoring the fact that this would make God out to be a monster. Evolution is certainly the most brutal and inefficient process conceivable by which to accomplish "creation." Most leading evolutionary scientists see this clearly, and consider such theologians to be misguided at best.

> The proponents of teleological theories, for all their efforts, have been unable to find any mechanism (except supernatural ones) that can account for their postulated finalism. . . . The frequency of extinction in every geological period is another powerful argument against any finalistic trend toward perfection.[2]

---

[1] Bertrand Russell, *Religion and Science* (London: Oxford University Press, 1961), p. 73.
[2] Ernst Mayr, "Evolution, "*Scientific American*, vol. 239 (September 1978), p. 50.

> Judged by scientists and others, much philosophy of science has been downright irrelevant, at best a series of brilliant axiomatic games, more often pretentious nonsense.[3]

So why would a professing believer be enamored with such games and nonsense as these?

Charles Darwin himself, once at least a nominal believer in God (the only degree he ever got was as a divinity student), was forced by the very nature of evolutionary theory to realize that it was inconsistent with the concept of a wise and loving God. He stressed that, instead of man's bringing death into the world as the Bible teaches (Rom. 5:12), death brought man into the world. We note again that in the very last paragraph of his *Origin of Species*, he wrote this declaration:

> Thus, from the war of nature, from famine and death, the most exalted object which we are capable of conceiving, namely, the production of the higher animals, directly follows.[4]

A brilliant young biologist of the present generation, in her book *The Center of Life*, notes the heartless and mindless character of evolution:

> Evolution is a hard, inescapable mistress. There is just no room for compassion or good sportsmanship. Too many organisms are born, so, quite simply, a lot of them are going to have to die, because there isn't enough food and space to go around. You can be beautiful, fat, strong, but it might not matter. The only thing that does matter is whether you leave more children carrying your genes than the next person leaves. It's true whether you're a prince, a frog, or an American elm. Evolution is a future phenomenon. Are your genes going to be in the next generation? That is all that counts.[5]

This is the system that our illogical theologicals would seek to harmonize with Christianity! The essence of Darwinism is the survival of the fittest (or the most prolific) in a life-and-death struggle for

---

[3] June Goodfield, "Humanity in Science," *Phi Beta Kappa Key Reporter* (Summer 1977), p. 4.

[4] Charles Darwin, *Origin of Species.* All editions, final paragraph.

[5] Lorraine Lee Larison Cudmore, excerpts as quoted in *Science Digest*, vol. 82 (November 1977), p. 46.

existence, with extermination of the weak and unfit. The Lord Jesus Christ, on the other hand, stressed that love and self-sacrifice, with special concern for the weak and helpless, must characterize true Christianity.

Evolutionism is compatible with communism, with fascism, with anarchism, imperialism, and all other systems based on struggle and hatred, but not with Christianity. It is a necessary component of atheism and materialism, but a very unnatural adjunct to theism.

> Marx admired [Darwin's] book not for economic reasons but for the more fundamental one that Darwin's universe was purely materialistic, and the explication of it no longer involved any reference to unobservable, non-material causes outside or "beyond" it. In that important respect, Darwin and Marx were truly comrades.[6]

It is bad enough for theological "liberals" to embrace evolutionism, but absolutely inexcusable for those who profess to believe the Bible and to follow Christ. Yet there have been many Christian leaders ever since Darwin who have led multitudes down this path of compromise and eventual apostasy, and the same cycle is repeating itself in much of so-called evangelicalism today.

The so-called "main line" churches and religious schools have long since capitulated to evolutionism and the religious liberalism that inevitably follows.

The modern creationist revival has caused great distress to this influential group. Ever since Darwin, a significant number of Christian clergymen and Christian intellectuals have felt it essential to be in line with "modern" thought and have, therefore, tried to accommodate evolution in their theology. Many of the greatest preachers of the 19th century — such as Henry Drummond in England and Henry Ward Beecher in America — soon were leading large numbers of their followers into theistic evolution, and it wasn't long before practically all the seminaries and colleges of the mainline denominations had capitulated to what they considered to be modern science.

Most people have the impression that the religionists of Darwin's day opposed evolutionism, while the scientists promoted it, with the resulting conflict being a classic example of religious bigotry opposing science, but it was really the other way around. The original and most vigorous opposition to Darwin came from scientists, whereas many

[6] Tom Bethell, "Burning Darwin to Save Marx," *Harper's* (December 1978), p. 37.

religious leaders were ready to accommodate "evolution" right from the start. Francis Glasson says:

> Darwin expected that his book would arouse violent criticism from the scientific world, and it certainly came from that quarter. According to his own account, most of the leading scientists of the day believed in the immutability of species. . . . On the other hand, many Christian leaders took a very different line, even from the early stages . . . Owen Chadwick, Regius Professor of Modern History at Cambridge, wrote after extensive research: "At first much of the opposition to Darwin's theory came from scientists on grounds of evidence, not from theologians on grounds of Scripture."[7]

The same has been true ever since, and is certainly true today. Almost all college and seminary faculty members of the large denominations teach theistic evolution.

Evangelical Compromise

The evolutionary philosophy thoroughly dominates the curricula and faculties of secular colleges and universities today, as well as the schools of the large religious denominations. It is not so well known, however, that this philosophy has also had considerable effect on many evangelical Christian colleges. When this fact is pointed out, the reaction of many Christians is one of surprise or even doubt. "How could . . . College, so well known for academic leadership in the Christian world, *possibly* be teaching evolution, especially when its faculty members all assent to a statement of faith? Surely there must be some mistake!"

There is no mistake, however. Although there are still many Christian schools whose faculties are strongly biblical and strictly creationist, many of the most highly respected schools have compromised with evolutionism to an alarming degree. An article entitled "Creationism and Evolutionism as Viewed in Consortium Colleges"[8] documented this fact quite thoroughly more than 20 years ago. Written by Dr. Albert J. Smith, a biology teacher at Wheaton College, this paper gives the views of 38 teachers in science and math from the Christian College Consortium, a group of about 10 or 12 of the leading Christian colleges, including such schools as Wheaton College, Gordon College,

---

[7] Francis Glasson, "Darwin and the Church," *New Scientist*, vol. 99 (September 1, 1983), p. 638–639.

[8] J. Albert Smith, "Creationism and Evolutionism as Viewed in Consortium Colleges," *Universitas*, vol. 2, no. 1 (March 1974).

Westmont College, Messiah College, Malone College, Taylor University, Seattle Pacific College, Greenville College, Bethel College, and Eastern Mennonite College.

Dr. Smith pointed out that, in the opinion of their own science faculties, these institutions have *no well-defined position* on creation or evolution. Nevertheless, these people also say that their institutions must "maintain a conservative stance for promotional purposes." Interesting! Financial supporters of Christian schools are usually strong creationists.

As far as the faculty members themselves were concerned, Dr. Smith says:

> Efforts to characterize and identify with the departmental positions results in all respondents calling themselves "theistic evolutionists," "progressive creationists," or infrequently "fiat creationists."[9]

It is good to know that there are still a few "fiat creationists" in the consortium, but it is evident that they constitute a small minority. "Progressive creationism," of course, is a semantic variant of "theistic evolutionism," both systems adopting the geologic-age framework that is essentially synonymous with naturalistic uniformitarianism, and rejecting the straightforward biblical teaching of a completed recent creation and worldwide Flood.

None of the colleges in the consortium openly teach evolutionism in the manner of secular colleges, of course. Some teachers do try to present both creation and evolution, and the evidences for and against each, to their students. The predominant attitude, however, is apparently that the question of origins is unimportant and irrelevant!

> Relatively few colleges emphasize the creationist-evolutionist dialogue at all. . . . The students are encouraged to make up their own minds regarding personal position.[10]

Quotations given in the article from the individual responses of faculty members show that many of them use the standard clichés in trying to avoid this question: ". . . creationism (a biblical statement) and evolutionism (a scientific statement) are not considered to be antagonistic but rather at different levels; creationism considers the *who* and the *why*, whereas evolution considers the *how*, the *when*, and the *how much*"; ". . . the important thing is not *how* but *Who.*"

---

[9] *Ibid.*

[10] *Ibid.*

The reason that true creationists object to such views, of course, is because the Bible *does* say how, when, and how much, *as well as* who and why! Furthermore, as the scientists of the Creation Research Society and the Institute for Creation Research have shown, the true facts of science do correlate much better with these biblical statements on creation than with evolution. Such facts, however, seem always to be ignored by "Christian evolutionists" and "progressive creationists."

Saying that the evolution/creation question is "not a significant problem," "not basic to the Christian faith," "unimportant," "a dead issue," and the like (all these judgments are quoted from respondents of the consortium) is most likely merely a devious way of saying: "Well, acceptance in the academic world requires me to believe in evolution, and I don't want to face up to the biblical and scientific reasons for rejecting evolution, so I would prefer to bypass the problem."

On one occasion several years ago, one of the writers (H. Morris) spent several hours discussing this problem with a professor of geology at one of the consortium colleges. This teacher insisted that Christians *must* accept the geological-age system as taught by evolutionary geologists. When asked how he, as a professedly Bible-believing Christian, reconciled the Genesis record of creation and the Flood with this system, his reply was that he didn't know of any way in which they *could* be reconciled (he agreed that neither the gap theory nor the day-age theory was acceptable). When also asked how he reconciled Jesus Christ's acceptance of the literal Genesis record of creation and the Flood with the geological ages, he replied that he didn't know how to reconcile that either. His final conclusion was that all of this was unimportant. Only one thing apparently *was* important; namely, to accept the geological ages (and to be acceptable to his secular peers)!

More recently, this writer had two opportunities to talk at some length with the head of the geology department at this college on the same subject. He took much the identical position, also adding that we would never be able to understand the meaning of the Genesis record of creation and the Flood until we get to heaven! It is not important for us to understand it now, he felt.

One must confess a certain lack of patience with this type of logic. How can a Christian say the doctrine of special creation is unimportant when it is foundational to every other doctrine in Scripture? How can one say the evolutionary philosophy is not significant, when it has been made the basis of Fascism, Communism, animalism, racism, modernism, atheism, and practically every other harmful philosophy known to man? How can *Christian* college professors teach their students that evolution is an optional question when the Scriptures plainly teach otherwise?

> "How long halt ye between two opinions? If the Lord be God, follow him: but if Baal, then follow him" (1 Kings 18:21).

Although evolutionism has most affected Christian higher education, this philosophy has also influenced numerous Christian elementary and secondary schools. Many leading Christian periodicals have, likewise, been significantly infiltrated by evolutionary thinking. A number of churches, missions, and other Christian institutions have been similarly affected.

One of the most frustrating problems encountered in trying to encourage and strengthen belief in a Creator and in creationism is the indifference of so many professing Christian people to the urgent importance of this issue. "I don't believe in evolution anyhow, so why should I waste time in studying or promoting creationism?" "Why get involved in peripheral and controversial issues like that — just preach the gospel!" "The Bible is not a textbook of science, but of how to live." "It is the Rock of Ages which is important — not the age of rocks!" "Winning souls is the principal thing — not the winning of debates."

Platitudes such as the above, however spiritual they sound, are really cop-outs. They tend to become excuses for avoiding serious thought and the offense of the cross. In the name of evangelism and of appealing to large numbers, a least-common-denominator emphasis on emotional experiences and a nominal commitment of some kind has become the dominant characteristic of most Christian teaching and activity today, and this is almost as true in fundamentalist and conservative circles as it is among religious liberals.

This ostrich-like attitude seems to date largely from the aftereffect of the infamous Scopes Trial in 1925. The fundamentalists and creationists were made to look so ridiculous by the news media covering that trial at the time (and they still are exploiting it today!) that Christians in general retreated altogether from the battle for the schools and for the minds of the young people. Avoiding any further attempt to relate science and history to an inspired and inerrant Bible, Christian teachers and preachers thenceforth emphasized evangelism and the spiritual life almost exclusively. The "gap theory," which supposedly allowed the earth's billions of years of evolutionary history to be pigeonholed between the first two verses of Genesis and then ignored, provided a convenient device for saying that the entire question was irrelevant.

As a consequence, in less than a generation the entire public school system and the very establishment itself — educational, scientific, political, military, industrial, and religious — was taken over by the evolutionary philosophy and its fruits of naturalism, humanism, socialism, and animalistic amoralism.

For the past several decades, of course, a noteworthy revival of creationism has been taking place, both in the churches and, to some extent, in the schools. Thousands of scientists have become creationists, and the interest among teachers and students in creationism is higher than it has ever been.

Nevertheless, although many churches and Christian people have become actively involved in the creation issue, it is still sadly true that the majority of them are indifferent, or even antagonistic, to creationism. They think that it is only a peripheral biological question, of no concern in the preaching of the gospel. Even most fundamentalists, who themselves believe in creation, think that evolution is a dead issue.

Such an attitude is based on wishful thinking, to say the least. The lead article some years ago in *Science*, the official journal of the prestigious American Association for the Advancement of Science, said the following:

> While many details remain unknown, the grand design of biologic structure and function in plants and animals, including men, admits to no other explanation than that of evolution. Man, therefore is another link in a chain which unites all life on this planet.[11]

Not only did man evolve, but so did "the religions of Jesus and Buddha."[12] That being so, not only are the supernatural aspects of Christianity open to question, but so are its ethical teachings.

> An ethical system that bases its premises on absolute pronouncements will not usually be acceptable to those who view human nature by evolutionary criteria.[13]

Ethics and morals must evolve as well as organisms! And so must social and political systems. There are no absolutes!

This is the logical and inevitable outgrowth of evolutionary teach-

---

[11] A. G. Motulsky: "Brave New World," *Science*, vol. 185 (August 23, 1974), p. 653.
[12] *Ibid.*
[13] *Ibid.*, p. 654.

ing. But it is also the logical and inevitable outgrowth of Christian indifference to evolutionary teaching.

The doctrine of special creation is the foundation of all other Christian doctrine. The experience of belief in Christ as Creator is the basis of all other Christian experience. Creationism is not peripheral or optional; it is central and vital! That is why God placed the account of creation at the beginning of the Bible, and why the very first verse of the Bible speaks of the creation of the physical universe.

Jesus Christ was Creator (Col. 1:16) before He became Redeemer (Col. 1:20). He is the very "beginning of the creation of God" (Rev. 3:14). How then can it be possible to really know Him as Saviour unless one also, and first, knows the triune God as Creator?

The very structure of man's time commemorates over and over again, week by week, the completed creation of all things in six days. The preaching of the gospel necessarily includes the preaching of creation: "The everlasting gospel to preach unto them that dwell on the earth . . . worship Him that made heaven, and earth, and the sea, and the fountains of waters" (Rev. 14:6-7).

If man is a product of evolution, he is not a fallen creature in need of a Saviour, but a rising creature, capable of saving himself.

> The ethical human brain is the highest accomplishment of biologic evolution.[14]

The gospel of evolution is the enemy of the gospel of Christ. The gospel of Christ leads to salvation, righteousness, joy, peace, and meaning in life. Evolution's gospel yields materialism, collectivism, anarchism, atheism, and despair in death.

Evolutionary thinking dominates our schools today — our news media, our entertainment, our politics, our entire lives. But evolution is false and absurd scientifically! How long will Christian people and churches remain ignorant and apathetic concerning it?

Christians who have been indifferent to the menace of evolution should consider the following analysis by Dr. William Provine, who is both professor of history and professor of biological sciences at Cornell University.

> As Jacques Monod, E. O. Wilson, and many other biologists have pointed out, modern evolutionary biology has shattered the hope that some kind of designing or purposive force guided human evolution and established

[14] *Ibid*, p. 662.

> the basis of moral rules. Instead, biology leads to a wholly mechanistic view of life. . . . There are no gods and no designing forces. The frequently made assertion that modern biology and assumptions of the Judeo-Christian tradition are fully compatible is false. Second, there exist no inherent moral or ethical laws, no absolute guiding principles for human society.[15]

If Provine and all his humanistic colleagues are right (that is, if evolution is true), then Christianity (or any other theistic religion) is redundant, or even harmful.

> Religion is like the human appendix: although it was functional in our distant ancestors, it is of no use today. Just as the appendix today is a focus of physical disease, so too religion today is a focus of social disease. Although religion was a force accelerating human evolution during the Ice Age, it is now an atavism of negative value.[16]

The above opinion is that of the former chairman of the division of science and technology at one of the colleges of the State University of New York (and himself a former "Christian"). In any case, his conclusion is quite sound if his premise is valid. That is, if evolution is true, then the Christian religion is false and, for the good of further evolutionary progress, the sooner it can be forgotten, the better.

But we can be thankful that evolution is *not* true! As shown in Volume II of this trilogy, the real facts of science support creation. The entire premise and framework of evolutionism is altogether false and its impact in human life and thought has been devastatingly harmful! Evangelical Christians urgently need to become informed and concerned and active in the battle to rebuild biblical creationism as the foundation of all truth and life, and no such compromise as progressive creationism can do this.

Current Evangelicalism

For a thorough refutation of all these compromise theories (gap theory, day-age theory, local flood theory, etc.), the reader is referred to

---

[15] William Provine, "Influence of Darwin's Ideas on the Study of Evolution," *Bioscience*, vol. 32 (June 1982), p. 506.

[16] Frank R. Zindler, "Religion, Hypnosis and Music: An Evolutionary Perspective," *American Atheist*, vol. 26 (October 1984), p. 24.

[17] See especially Henry M. Morris's *Biblical Creationism* (Grand Rapids, MI: Baker Book House, 1993), in which every passage in the Bible dealing with creation, the Flood, or related issues is examined.

Volume 1 of this Trilogy. Many earlier books, by these writers and others, published especially in the last 30 years, have documented this biblical evidence over and over again.[17] The biblical record, as clearly and unequivocally as could possibly be expressed in human language, teaches that all things were created supernaturally by God in six literal days several thousand years ago, and the same is true of the cataclysmic global Flood in the days of Noah. Like it or not, that *is* what God has said in His Word!

However, the old cycle of compromise is again repeating itself. In reaction against the revival of scientific, literal biblical creationism that has been convincing millions around the world in recent decades, including thousands of fully qualified scientists, a number of evangelical scientists have been vigorously attacking those of us whom they call "young-earth creationists." Insisting that Christians must accept the supposed scientific evidence of the "Big Bang" origin of the universe around 15 billion years ago, as well as the 4.5 billion years of "geological ages" of earth history, in order to be approved by the scientific community, they want to be recognized as "progressive creationists" by the Christian community.

A number of books have been published in recent years by such men, often sarcastically disparaging the scientific sophistication of young-earth creationists, and then trying to reinterpret the Scriptures to accommodate their "old-earth creationism." The most influential of these writers has been Dr. Hugh Ross, who has a Ph.D. in astronomy (University of Toronto) and heads an organization called "Reasons to Believe." Apart from a post-doctoral stint at the California Institute of Technology, Ross has apparently contributed little to the science of astronomy itself. Nevertheless, he frequently insists that all Christians should accept his astronomical expertise in assuring us that the "Big Bang" represents — is equivalent to — the divine creation of the universe as stated in Genesis 1:1.

The great majority of leading astronomers, of course, disagree emphatically with this. Many reject the Big-Bang hypothesis altogether — men such as Sir Fred Hoyle, Hannes Alfven, Geoffrey Burbidge, Halton Arp, Eric Lerner, and many others. Those who do accept it (and they currently represent the majority), with few exceptions consider the Big Bang as a purely naturalistic occurrence, as a quantum fluctuation from primeval nothingness, or something of the sort.

Nevertheless, evangelicals seem to be falling all over themselves in scrambling onto the Hugh Ross bandwagon today. His teachings have been promoted not only by numerous leading churches and Christian colleges, but also by the Navigators, Campus Crusade for Christ, Inter-Varsity Christian Fellowship, the Gideons International,[18] Ligonier Ministries, Focus on the Family, Trinity Broadcast Network, and many others.

Dr. Ross's imposition of Scripture on the sciences of astronomy and cosmology is accepted by few if any leading scholars in these fields. But it is his distortions of Scripture that are of greater concern to us "young earth creationists," upon whom he looks with such patronizing disdain.

In order to accept the standard Big-Bang system of stellar and cosmic evolution, Dr. Ross then must accept the geological ages with their billions of years of suffering and death in the animal kingdom. This, of course, requires him also to accept the local flood theory and pre-Adamic man-like creatures, who looked and acted like human beings but had no eternal souls.

All of this obviously requires such distortion of Scripture as to amount in effect to a rejection of its inerrancy and clarity. Hugh Ross still insists that he is a "creationist," and he does hold to the traditional doctrines of evangelical Christianity (the deity of Christ, substitutionary atonement, etc.). He is actively evangelistic, an attribute which no doubt contributes to his wide acceptance and promotion by evangelicals.[19] The fact remains, however, that his system of biblical interpretation is grievously in error,[20] and is leading many unwary Christians down the same wide path to liberal unbelief that has been followed by multitudes of professing Christians in previous generations.

Dr. Ross is not by any means the only "progressive creationist" opposing literal biblical creationism, of course. Other influential books

[18] Dr. Ross was featured speaker at a recent International Convention of the Gideons, and his message was then featured in the monthly *Gideon* magazine. When one of us (H. Morris) objected and offered to submit a paper, defending recent creation as a matter of balance, he was refused. He had been a member of the Gideons since 1942, was formerly a state president of the Gideons, and had prepared many of the "Helps" in the Gideon Bibles, so this rejection was hard to understand. We hope that this decision to follow the Ross compromise doesn't presage a drift of the Gideons away from their love for God's Word.

[19] We have been rebuked by Rossites for an "unloving" attitude toward a Christian brother. The fact is, however, that Dr. Ross has devoted far more space in his writings and time in his lectures to denigrating young-earth creationists in general, and us in particular.

[20] A number of articles have discussed this fact in detail. See especially the book *Creation and Time,* by Paul Taylor and Mark Van Bebber (Films for Christ, 1994). The entire book is devoted to an exposition of Ross's faulty interpretations and misapplications of Scripture and early Christian writers.

in this vein have been written by Dr. Davis Young, Dr. Pattle P.T. Pun, Dr. Robert Gange, Dr. Robert Newman, Alan Hayward, Don Stoner, and others. Still others, more in the frank genre of theistic evolution, have come from Howard Van Till, Richard Bube, and others. Most of the scientists in the American Scientific Affiliation and in England's Victoria Institute are either theistic evolutionists or progressive creationists, as are the science faculties at Wheaton College, Gordon-Conwell College, Westmont College, Point Loma College, and many other leading evangelical colleges.

In the early days of this country, the schools and colleges were committed to Scripture and the Christian gospel, including true creationism. But great institutions such as Harvard, Yale, Brown, and others soon capitulated to unitarianism and then to evolutionism, finally becoming bastions of atheism, Marxism and (more recently) New Age pantheism. Later, notable denominational schools (Baylor, Southern Methodist, Princeton, Notre Dame, etc.) went through the same decline, though still maintaining a very tenuous commitment to their respective denominational tenets.

Now we also find evangelical schools, founded mostly in the present century with the purpose of returning to sound biblical doctrinal standards, repeating the same old compromising cycle. Even the charismatic and "fundamentalist" schools have been affected, many of them advocating the so-called "gap theory," which tries to retain the evolutionary ages of geology and astronomy by inserting them in an imaginary "gap" of billions of years prior to Genesis 1:2. This compromise is even less defensible scientifically than the day-age theory of the progressive creationists.

The tragedy is that all such compromises with evolutionism are utterly unwarranted! There is *no* scientific evidence for evolution in the first place, nor any *real* scientific evidence for the great age of the earth as demanded by evolutionists. All of this is discussed in detail in Volume 2 of this Trilogy.

Furthermore, as shown in *this* book, evolutionism has provided the pseudo-scientific rationale for nearly every deadly philosophy and evil practice known to man! By all that is right and good in this world, and by God's Word, evolution simply *cannot* be true, and Christians ought to oppose and repudiate it in all of its disguises, not compromise with it.

Evolutionism, thus, has impacted society in many, many areas, including religion, even evangelicalism and fundamentalism. The Bible makes it clear that Satan, the father of lies (John 8:44), is the one who has deceived the whole world (Rev. 12:9). By various and devious means, all through history and in every nation, he has sought to keep men from knowing the true God of creation and redemption, and also to confuse and dissuade and discourage those who do know Him. He has used the deceptive lure of evolution, in one form or another, as a substitute for the Creator, with the ultimate aim of eventually dethroning God and usurping His cosmic kingdom for himself.

He will be defeated, of course, and eventually confined forever in the lake of fire (Rev. 20:10), with all who have chosen and worshipped his substitute "god" over the true God. The great Deceiver has deceived multitudes, to their eternal doom, but he has deceived himself most of all.

Index of Subjects

Index of Names

Index of Scripture